IMMERSION IN MORMONISM

By Charles Abbott

To Ashley
from Charles Abbott

This book is dedicated to my wife,
Oranee, who is the love of my life—
and to my family.

I also wish to thank our friends, Rodger and Virginia Galland, James Jackson, Scott Nyman and Gordon Robinson, and my children and their spouses, who reviewed various drafts of the manuscript and made valuable suggestions. While I followed many of them, I did not follow all of them and consequently must take full responsibility for the thoughts expressed herein and for any errors. Please know also that this book is not published or sponsored in any way by the Church of Jesus Christ of Latter-Day Saints.

CONTENTS

INTRODUCTION

I joined The Church of Jesus Christ of Latter-day Saints[1] when I was twenty years old. It was the best decision I have ever made in my life. Why? Because through my membership in the Church I have been blessed with everything that is really important. But when I joined the Church I did not fully understand what it took to receive those blessings.

I have targeted my message to converts. Who are converts? Everyone who is a member, if they are to be active, must become a convert at one point or another in their life as they develop a testimony of their own. And then it is a lifelong process to keep their testimony intact and make it grow even stronger.

---

1. Because it makes for easier reading we'll generally just shorten references to the Church by using the term "LDS Church" or simply "the Church" with a capitalized "C" rather than its full name.

We all face challenges, hardships and temptations that may impact our faith. For example, recent converts may find it difficult to adapt to a new and different lifestyle. Teenagers and other young people must make decisions about standards and values that will govern their lives while at the same time resisting peer pressure and the constant presence of harmful Internet material that invades our homes, our computers and even our phones. And Satan never gives up on us, even as we age. The path to an unshakable testimony is one we must follow for all of our lives.

Baptism is just the beginning. Obtaining the full benefits of membership takes effort, and you may even need to give up a few things. But I guarantee you that it is all worth it. The blessings of full immersion in the programs of the Church will more than compensate you for your effort and for anything you have had to give up.

I should add that it is my hope that this book will also wind up in the hands of investigators and persons who are curious about the Church. Gaining a clearer understanding of the immediate and eternal blessings to self and loved ones that can flow from immersion in the doctrines of the Church just might be the "tipping point" for some of them if they are investigators.

In the first chapter I will begin with a short discussion of my own conversion when I was twenty, recognizing that we are all different and it is quite likely that your path to conversion may be very different than mine. As I have said, the real focus of my message is to discuss the benefits of total immersion in the Church programs after baptism. My goal is to show you how you can attain everything that is really important in this life and in the life that follows. Does that sound too good to be true? Does it sound like I am exaggerating? Well, I'm not. But if you think I might be, then read this book to the end. If you still feel that way, then send me an email and tell me where I went wrong. And if you decide to put any of this into practice, email me and tell me if it worked or if it didn't work. But don't wait too long. I'm 76 years old, and the email address I will give you near the end of this book will expire when I expire.

Before we begin our discussion I need to clarify a few things:

First, the Church structure and programs I am about to describe are based on fully developed wards and branches of the Church. I am aware of the fact that in some places, where a branch is in a beginning stage with only a few members, all of the things I am about to describe are not fully developed. If you live in such an area, that would make your involvement and assistance even more important. Perhaps you could help build up the membership by referring some friends to the missionaries. As a former President of the Church, David O. McKay, instructed us, "Every member a missionary!"

Second, as I will discuss in much more detail later, there are certain changes you may have to make in your life. Just for example, if you are accustomed to going to bars on Friday nights or playing golf every Sunday, this will no longer be compatible with your new lifestyle. As a result you may lose the companionship of some good friends. That does not mean that you can't associate with people who do such things. We have many good friends who are not members of our church and we respect them no less because at dinner they may be having a glass of wine while we sip our 7-Ups. But as a result of your joining the Church you may not have as much in common with some of your friends. They may think you are crazy to have made the sacrifices you will have made to join the Church, but perhaps you can help them understand why you did it. Luke 22:32 states, "And when thou art converted, strengthen thy brethren." Perhaps you can persuade some of them to talk to the missionaries, at least so they can understand why you have made some different choices in your life. And maybe they will never understand why you have chosen to join this church and perhaps they will not enjoy your company as much. But regardless of how all of that turns out, just know that you will gain some new friends and new activities that will bless your life. More about that later.

Third, at some point and maybe even soon, some member of the Church (and even someone with a leadership position in the Church) may say or do something that offends you. I know of some people who have become inactive because of that. Please, just shake it off. It happens. No one is perfect and if someone offends you on purpose the fault is theirs, not yours. And it is certainly not the fault of the Church. In fact, our leaders teach us *not* to offend people but instead to love people, and more often than not those teachings are taken to heart. But we are all just human and sometimes we say or do something that is offensive to someone.

Years ago, when I was serving in the bishopric of a ward, I gave a talk in church. At 2:00 in the morning I was awakened by a phone call from a very good friend who was in the congregation and heard my remarks. He said, "Chuck, I have always been taught that I should never go to bed angry with someone. I have been struggling to go to sleep but can't, because something you said offended me. I am calling you now to talk to you about it." We did talk and he came to know that he had misunderstood my remarks and that while I might have worded them a bit better I certainly didn't intend to offend him or anyone else for that matter. As a result of his call we are still dear friends to this day and we both learned valuable lessons from the experience. He learned that if you are offended it is most probable that the person who offended you didn't mean it. I learned that I should be more careful about what I say and how I say it, and also that a person should never go to bed angry with someone.

Fourth, as time goes on you may come across arguments challenging the Church's teachings or practices. Sometimes they sound pretty convincing—that is, until you examine the motives or beliefs of the parties who make them or the underlying factual assumptions upon which they are based. We'll go into more detail about how to deal with that later.

Fifth, please forgive me if I cover some things you already know. I just don't know how much you know, especially if you have recently joined the Church. I remember how it was with me when I first joined. I was sitting in a sacrament meeting and the bishop announced that we would meet the following Sunday at the stake house. I thought to myself, "Oh boy, I joined the right church. We're meeting at the steak house on Sunday for a steak dinner!" Fortunately my girl friend (later to become my wife) set me straight.

Sixth, please know that this book is not an official publication of The Church of Jesus Christ of Latter-day Saints or sponsored by the Church in any way. My wife has helped me bring my thoughts all together in publishable form. A few of our friends have read the manuscript and made suggestions, and I have even followed many of them. However, I didn't follow all of them, and so if there are errors I can blame no one but myself.[2]

2. Throughout this book I will use some terms that are part of our Mormon culture but which may be less familiar to new members, at least in the context in which we use them. At the end of the book is a glossary to help clarify those terms.

CHAPTER ONE

MY CONVERSION

I grew up in Sedro-Woolley, Washington, then a small town of about 3700 people, located about 60 miles north of Seattle. There were only a handful of Mormons in our town. I knew nothing about them.

During the summer just before my freshman year of college at the University of Washington a girl named Oranee Harward[3] moved from Utah into our town to live with her older brother and his wife for a few months. She was next to the youngest of ten children. Her father had died when she was less than a year old and her mother struggled to earn enough money to raise

---

3. The name Oranee is an unusual one and most people mispronounce it until they learn that it is the combination of two names. Her father's name was Oran and her mother's name was Renee'. So, combining those two names gave them Oranee, pronounced "Or-uh-nay."

the children. Finally her mother had arranged to take a course in nursing in Colorado so she could develop skills that would earn her more money. While she did that she farmed the younger children out to live with their older siblings.

As fate would have it, Oranee's brother, Tom, and his wife, Catherine, shared a home in Sedro-Woolley with Catherine's father and mother. Together they ran a successful restaurant. The home was also occupied by Catherine's younger brother, George, who was my best friend. Oranee was 15 years old, going on 16, and a junior in high school. I was only 17. I didn't know it at the time, but Oranee's moving into that home turned out to be the luckiest day of my life. George and I ran around with some good kids, the few who didn't drink, use drugs, or engage in inappropriate sexual relationships. Oranee fit right into that group. She was the nicest girl I had ever met. She was also attractive—and she was a lot of fun. As I said, my lucky day.

In the beginning there was no particular romantic interest for the simple reason that I didn't think I stood a chance. But with our group of compatible friends we went water-skiing in the summer and snow-skiing in the winter, and gradually began to fall in love. She was a Mormon and I was an Episcopalian. I should add that I was very happy with my Episcopalian membership and continue to have fond memories of it. When my mother and father had moved to town before I was born my mother felt there was not a "proper church" for her children to attend, so she got together with some other women and raised money to purchase a very nice church building. They hired a minister and established the St. James Episcopal Church in Sedro-Woolley. They bought a pipe organ from the local theater. In the early days it had been used to accompany silent movies, but now that there were talkies it was no longer needed. The neat thing about the organ was that, unlike most church organs, it had cymbals and drums and trumpets and trombones. The very nice minister they hired happened to be a jazz musician and so sometimes he would do jazz concerts on the organ in the middle of the week.

Nevertheless, our family did not attend church regularly and the doctrines of the church were not a dominant force in our daily lives. We attended about once a month, for an hour, and always on Easter and Christmas Eve. One of my fondest memories is of when our church put on a play for the whole town, showcased in the downtown movie theater. It was called *They Went Thataway*. It was about some cowboys, and at 15 years of age I played the romantic lead simply because they couldn't find any adults willing to do it. Before that I had kissed only one girl (on her cheek and when we were both six years old). So, in this play at the very end I had to kiss a girl. If that wasn't traumatic enough, she was 35 years old, married, and a secretary in the furniture store where I worked. It was one of the grossest things I have ever been asked to do—or at least I thought so then. Fortunately I wasn't traumatized for life and now I can look back at the experience with a feeling of some amusement.

As a freshman at the University of Washington I became exposed to a lot of new ideas—things I had never thought about before. I took classes in subjects such as economics, philosophy, and sociology. As my intellectual curiosity was awakened, I began to think about religion. Mainly, I wondered what my church believed, and whether I believed it. So I went down to the stacks at the university library, found the shelves where the books on religion were kept, and began to select a few to read.

As I was picking over these books I ran across one called *A Marvelous Work and a Wonder*, by LeGrand Richards, an LDS Apostle. It was about the LDS Church. Oranee and I were not "going steady" or anything like that. We just hung out as part of a large group of friends. She was very active in her church, and she had told me some things about it. I said to myself, "Oranee is the nicest girl I have ever met, and she is a Mormon—I wonder what they believe." I never would have taken that book off the shelf if I had not met her. And so I checked it out along with books about Methodists, Presbyterians, Catholics, Episcopalians, and other churches. What I learned is that there are many areas of disagreement among the Christian churches.

I was very struck with a statement in the beginning of *A Marvelous Work and a Wonder*:

> "Many years ago a learned man, a member of the Roman Catholic Church, came to Utah and spoke from the stand of the Salt Lake Tabernacle. I became well-acquainted with him, and we conversed freely and frankly. A great scholar, with perhaps a dozen languages at his tongue's end, he seemed to know all about theology, law, literature, science and philosophy. One day he said to me: 'You Mormons are all ignoramuses. You don't even know the strength of your own position. It is so strong that there is only one other tenable in the whole Christian world, and that is the position of the Catholic Church. The issue is between Catholicism and Mormonism. If we are right, you are wrong; if you are right, we are wrong; and that's all there is to it. The Protestants haven't a leg to stand on. For, if we are wrong, they are wrong with us, since they

> were a part of us and went out from us; while if we are right, they are apostates whom we cut off long ago. If we have the apostolic succession from St. Peter, as we claim, there is no need of Joseph Smith and Mormonism; but if we have not that succession, then such a man as Joseph Smith was necessary, and Mormonism's attitude is the only consistent one. It is either the perpetuation of the gospel from ancient times, or the restoration of the gospel in latter days'" (LeGrand Richards, *A Marvelous Work and a Wonder*, p. 3).

This statement tweaked my curiosity. I determined right then and there to try to find out which of the many churches was right. As I studied the beliefs of the various churches I learned that the doctrine of the Trinity, which has been accepted in one form or another by the Catholics and most of the Protestants, was the result of a political compromise engineered by Constantine, the emperor of the Roman Empire, in the city of Nicea in A.D. 325. Constantine wasn't even a Christian, but instead was a sun-worshiper. However, in trying to unify the Roman Empire he felt it was important to reach some sort of unity among warring factions of the Christian church. Arias, who was a priest from Egypt, was teaching his many followers that, because Christ was the son of God, He was a being who was created by the Father and therefore was younger than the Father and a separate being. Athanasius, who was a priesthood holder from Egypt and who also had many followers, was teaching that the Father, the Son and the Holy Ghost were one eternal being existing co-eternally, but at the same time were separate and distinct from each other. The doctrine of the Trinity was nothing more than an attempt to satisfy both factions by saying that the Godhead consists of one God who is also three Gods.

The doctrine of the Trinity, outlined in the "Nicene Creed," was later amplified by the Athanasian Creed, which has been widely accepted in varying forms since the sixth century as a foundation of their faith by many western Christian churches, including the Catholics, Lutherans, Methodists and others. The Athanasian Creed is as follows:

> We worship one God in Trinity, and Trinity in Unity; neither confounding the persons; nor dividing the substance. For there is one Person of the Father; another of the Son, and another of the Holy Ghost.
>
> But the Godhead of the Father, of the Son, and of the Holy Ghost, is all one: the Glory equal, the Majesty co-eternal. Such as the Father is, so is the Son, and such is the Holy Ghost.
>
> The Father uncreate, the Son uncreate, and the

Holy Ghost uncreate. The Father incomprehensible, and the Holy Ghost incomprehensible. The Father eternal, the Son eternal, and the Holy Ghost eternal.

And yet there are not three eternals, but one eternal. Also there are not three incomprehensibles, not three uncreated, but one uncreated, and one incomprehensible.

So likewise the Father is Almighty, the Son Almighty and the Holy Ghost Almighty. And yet there are not three Almighties, but one Almighty.

So the Father is God, the Son is God, and the Holy Ghost is God. And yet there are not three Gods, but one God.

So likewise the Father is Lord, the Son Lord, and the Holy Ghost Lord. And yet not three Lords but one Lord.

For like as we are compelled by the Christian verity to acknowledge every person by himself to be God and Lord; so we are forbidden by the Catholic religion to say, There be three Gods, or three Lords.

The Father is made of none; neither created, nor begotten. The Son is of the Father alone: Not made, nor created, but begotten. The Holy Ghost is of the Father and of the Son; neither made, nor created, nor begotten, but proceeding.

So there is one Father, not three Fathers, one Son, not three Sons: one Holy Ghost, not three Holy Ghosts.

> And of this Trinity none is afore, or after another, none is greater or less than others; but the whole three persons are co-eternal together; and co-equal. So that in all things as is aforesaid: the Unity in Trinity, and the Trinity in Unity is to be worshiped.
>
> He therefore that will be saved must thus think of the Trinity.[4]

From the scriptures I also learned that a great apostasy from the teachings of Christ had been predicted long before the Council of Nicea. Paul said, "For the time will come when they will not endure sound doctrine; but after their own lusts shall they heap to themselves teachers, having itching ears; and they shall turn away their ears from the truth, and shall be turned unto fables" (2 Timothy 4:3–4). "For I know this, that after my departing shall grievous wolves enter in among you, not sparing the flock. Also of your own selves shall men arise, speaking perverse things to draw away disciples after them" (Acts 20:29–30).

After studying these beliefs I was confused. I couldn't understand how God could be three

4. This version of the Athanasian Creed is just one of many, and if you are interested in seeing other versions just google "Athenasian Creed" on the Internet, and while you are at it you might wish to search for "List of Christian Creeds." There are many man-made variations of belief about basic Christian doctrines. They show why a restoration was needed.

beings but only one being. It seemed to me that if "God created man in his own image, in the image of God created he him," and if Paul confirmed this, declaring that Christ is in "the express image of his [God's] person," then it must follow that God did indeed have individual substance and form (Hebrews 1:3). I asked myself, "How could God create man in his image if God was not in the form of a person?"

In addition, I learned that there are numerous scriptures testifying of persons who saw God "face to face" and/or parts of his physical body. (See, for example: Genesis 5:24, 18:22, 32:30; 1 Corinthians 3:12; Revelation 22:4; Exodus 24:10, 31:18, 33:23; Numbers 12:8; Acts 7:55; Ezekiel 1:27; Revelation 19:12,15, 19:11,13; Isaiah 6:1; and Acts 7:55–57, where it is reported that Stephen, who being full of the Holy Ghost, was privileged to look up into heaven where he saw Jesus standing on the right hand of God.)

I learned that many churches place great emphasis on scriptural passages such as John 17:21–22, where Jesus prayed for his apostles and the saints: "That they all may be one; as thou, Father, art in me, and I in thee, that they also may be one in us; that the world may believe that thou hast sent me. And the glory which thou gavest me I have given them that they may be one, even as we are one." These churches say that this scriptural passage proves Jesus and His Father are one, but to me it seemed just the opposite. By praying that his followers would be "one" with Jesus and his Father in the same way He and His Father are one with each other, Jesus could not have meant that their beings would merge with those of Jesus and God the Father, but instead that they would be one in purpose in the same way Jesus and his Father were joined in purpose.

In addition, there were many scriptures that seemed to clearly indicate that the Godhead consisted of three separate beings. Just for example, Jesus said "I seek not mine own will, but the will of the Father which hath sent me" (John 5:30). He said, "My doctrine is not mine, but His that sent me" (John 7:16). And he said, "My Father is greater than I" (John 14:28).

While I was engaged in this study of the churches I happened to visit a sick friend who was recovering in a Catholic hospital. While I was waiting to be admitted to his room I spotted a Catholic Bible sitting on an end table next to my chair. I had learned about the unique Mormon practice of baptism for the dead and so I turned to 1 Corinthians 15:29 where Paul is teaching the people about the resurrection and says: "Else what shall they do which are baptized for the dead, if the dead rise not at all? Why are they then baptized for the dead?" There was a footnote in that Bible, and it said that this apparently refers to an early practice in the church which was discontinued in A.D. 325. To me this gave added credibility to claims that a restoration was needed.

Finally, my mother, who was opposed to my joining the LDS Church, sent me to the chaplain of the University of Washington, hoping he could talk some sense into my head. I asked him about 1 Corinthians 15:29, telling him that the Mormons practice baptism for the dead just as in the early days of the church. He was an ordained minister with a PhD in divinity. That's why his answer surprised me. He said, "I have never noticed that scripture before." Obviously he didn't talk me out of my investigation of the Church.

By this time Oranee had returned to Utah, but I was thoroughly in love and so managed to stay in touch and even get together from time to time. I saved and saved until I had about $250 and then I got Oranee a diamond engagement ring. I waited for an opportune time and one evening I drove to a romantic spot and popped the question: "Will you marry me?" She said, "No." So, I said, "Well then, I won't need this!" And I threw the ring out the window of the car and into the night. I wasn't angry. It was just that I was totally in love and didn't see how I could ever love anyone else—so I had no more need for the ring! Then she looked at me and she gently said, "But I might—sometime." We spent the next two hours crawling around on a grassy lawn, in the dark, looking for that tiny ring. Eventually we found it.

I was too clueless to know why she turned me down, and she didn't tell me why. It was because I wasn't a member of the Church and she wanted to be married in the temple. She was afraid that if she told me the reason she turned me down I would join the Church just so she'd marry me, but that I would not be totally converted to the doctrines and immersed in the lifestyle.

By then, through my study of the scriptures, including the Book of Mormon, I was motivated to investigate the Church even further, and so Oranee arranged an appointment for me to talk to some missionaries. After meeting with them a number of times I was even more convinced of the truth of what they were teaching. I was becoming converted intellectually. However, a testimony based solely on intellectual conversion can be fragile. As a lawyer, I know something about that. Practicing law I have learned that it is possible to make good sounding intellectual arguments on either side of any question. You can even make a good argument that there is no God at all. That's why there are so many atheists. And, while I don't think much of the arguments that support the doctrine of the Trinity as defined in the Nicene Creed,[5] I certainly realize that there are some very bright people who have and will make seemingly convincing arguments on it's behalf.

As those missionaries pointed out, a mere intellectual conversion can lead to a testimony that changes because someone comes along with a good sounding argument that causes doubt or a shift of your beliefs. Nevertheless, for most converts their path to membership does indeed begin with an intellectual conversion. Someone teaches them about the doctrines of the Church and the evidence that supports them, and they all make sense. But it is also important, and not just for converts, that all members of the Church commit the matter to prayer following the instructions found in the Book of Mormon at Moroni 10:4–5:

> And when ye shall receive these things, I would exhort you that ye would ask God, the Eternal Father, in the name of Christ, if these things are not true; and if ye shall ask with a sincere heart, with real intent, having faith in Christ, he will manifest the truth of it unto you, by the power of the Holy Ghost. And by the power of the

5. Or, for that matter, in the Apostles' Creed or the Athenasian Creed, which modified those doctrines even more.

Holy Ghost ye may know the truth of all things.

It is important to have a spiritual conversion instead of just an intellectual conversion. As you continue your activity in the Church you will find that there are many who seek to destroy your testimony by presenting what might seem to be good intellectual arguments.

After I began to believe, in a purely intellectual sense, that the Church was true I followed Moroni's instructions and committed the matter to prayer. I did not have a spectacular vision such as Joseph Smith had. The Holy Ghost did not shout at me but, answering my prayers, He whispered—and I came to feel in my heart that the restored gospel was true.

There are some people who come to "know" it is true the first time they ever pray about it. But that may not be typical. We are taught that our testimonies grow slowly "line upon line, precept upon precept" (see Isaiah 28:9–10) and, further, that "he that receiveth light, and continueth in God, receiveth more light"; and that the "light groweth brighter and brighter until the perfect day" (D&C 50:24). Over the years, as I have been immersed in the Church, the truth of its teachings has been reconfirmed and my testimony strengthened many times over, and the Holy Ghost has raised His voice above a whisper and even shouted at me more than once.

The important thing for us to know is that while our testimonies are growing we must continue to approach the Lord in faith. I know people who defiantly cross their arms across their chest, take a firm defensive stance, and then challenge the Lord to try to penetrate their defenses by showing them a miracle. It isn't likely to happen that way. Christ said, "Behold, I stand at the door, and knock: if any man hear my voice and open the door, I will come in to him" (Revelation 3:20). It is up to us to open the door and let him in. And while we are at it, we should also open our eyes. That is the role of faith, the first principle of the gospel.

I began this book by saying that through my membership in the Church I have been blessed with everything that is really important. It's true, and the blessings started immediately. It took me three years, but I finally joined the Church and then, miracle of all miracles, the next time I asked Oranee to marry me she said "yes." Since then she has been my mentor, not just bringing me into the Church but also showing me how to maximize the benefits of membership by immersing myself in the lifestyle.

But enough about me. Now I'd like to focus on you and show you what you need to do to realize the wonderful benefits that can come from your membership in The Church of Jesus Christ of Latter-day Saints.

I want to show you how being fully active in the Church can give them all to you. Membership in The Church of Jesus Christ of Latter-day Saints is more than just nominal membership in a church. It is a new way of life. But most important, it is a wonderful new way of life. To achieve the blessings that will flow from your membership in the Church requires more than mere membership—it is a process of immersing yourself totally into that new way of life.

CHAPTER 2

INSPIRED PROGRAMS

As you know, the Church has no paid ministry. One's first reaction on learning about that might be to think that we are shorthanded because we lack the benefit of a full-time preacher. However, as we examine the structure of the Church programs more closely we find that the typical ward is extraordinarily well staffed. The bishop (or branch president) and his two counselors will spend many hours each week in planning, structuring and administering the Church programs and counseling with members who need help. But they also have a lot of help from members of the congregation. Someone once told me, "The genius of the Mormon Church is its ability to get people to do for free that which they wouldn't do for pay." They thought they were joking but the fact is, it is true, and it is evidence (at least to me) that the gospel is true. It is just one more evidence that those who have organized these marvelous Church programs which bless our lives so abundantly are indeed inspired by our Heavenly Father.

Years ago, when a new meeting house was being built, the members would turn out with their hammers and saws to help. I remember a man who was inactive but who came to help on a building. He was a carpenter and wanted to contribute his talents. Working on the building gave him "ownership" of it. It became his building and, as a consequence, he and his family became active in the ward. That is exactly what serving in Church callings does for us. Immersion in these programs, not just as receivers but also as givers, gives us "ownership." It becomes "our church" in a deeply emotional way.

The Relief Society

I want to begin my description of Church organizations by describing the Relief Society. It is the largest women's organization in the world. While the men are being instructed in Sunday priesthood meetings by brethren who are called to teach them, the sisters are being instructed in their Relief Society meetings by sisters with similar callings. The Relief Society was organized by the

Prophet Joseph Smith in 1842. In defining the purpose of the Relief Society he said that it might provoke the brethren to good works in looking to the wants of the poor, in searching after objects of charity, and in administering to their wants, and by correcting the morals and strengthening the virtues of the female community.[6] His wife, Emma, was its first president.

There is no way to adequately describe the Relief Society and its members except to say that they are incredible. Their Sunday lessons are outstanding. But most important, the sisters are the ones we often turn to first when we have a need for loving service. The motto of the Relief Society is "Charity Never Faileth" and their purpose is to "prepare women for the blessings of eternal life by helping them increase their faith and personal righteousness, strengthen families and homes, and help those in need." They accomplish those purposes through Sunday gospel instruction, other Relief Society meetings during the week, monthly home visits, (called "visiting teaching") and welfare and compassionate service.

My wife had open heart surgery two years ago. She went to New York to have it done. A day or

---

6. This is from a discourse given by Joseph Smith in 1842, reported by Willard Richards in Relief Society, Minute Book, March 1842–March 1944, p. 7, Church Archives.

two before she was released from the hospital she was visited by a social worker who wanted to verify that she would have adequate help at home. He was not familiar with the Church or its programs. Oranee proceeded to tell him about what she could expect on her arrival home. She said the Relief Society would arrange to have its members bring in meals daily and for as long as needed. If I had to leave her alone and she needed help, they would come in and care for her. She told him about Relief Society "visiting teachers," assigned to visit our home at least monthly to serve us in any way they can. She said they would be visiting even more often during her recovery, to help her and to keep her spirits up. This social worker was absolutely amazed. He stayed and visited with her for an hour while she explained what it means to be a member of a church surrounded by neighbors who love and care for you as if you were part of their family. And when she came home everything that she predicted did indeed come to pass. As her husband I did my best to care for her, keeping our home picked up and clean, washing the clothes, etc. But it was so helpful to have those meals brought in for a couple of weeks and to have sisters visiting with Oranee while I tended to my chores or ran errands. It was also very helpful to have the tireless services of three loving daughters and a loving son, and their spouses, and our grandchildren, all of whom grew up immersed in programs where they learned to serve others.

Primary

For our young people it begins with Primary, where children from the ages of 3 through 11 begin learning gospel principles. It is led by a president and two counselors. These sisters coordinate and supervise the efforts of music leaders and of teachers for each of the age groups. Every Sunday the children learn songs with wonderful character-building messages, such as "I am a Child of God," and "Love at Home." They are taught lessons appropriate for their age where they learn the basic principles of the gospel. Even at this young age they are given opportunities to teach and speak and share their testimonies with others in their classes. The primary is staffed by volunteers, sometimes teenagers and young single adults, but more often by mothers and fathers. Following structured programs of the Church and under the direction of the Primary presidency the Primary leaders make it all fun with games and activities suitable to the age groups and which complement the lessons they are teaching. Just like the rest of the leaders, they are willing to serve without pay because they care, knowing also that they and their children will be similarly blessed by the volunteer efforts of others.

Young Men and Young Women Programs

But it does not end with Primary. When the children advance from Primary, they enter programs for young men and young women who are 12 through 17 years of age. Like the other programs of the Church, these programs are staffed by volunteers who serve because they love the Lord, they love to serve, and they love to help their children and the children of their good friends. Under the direction of these leaders, which includes young people in the group who share leadership responsibilities, the young men and women participate in lessons where they learn gospel principles and then get together in the middle of each week for enjoyable and wholesome activities including organized athletic events for those who would like to participate. Most important, they learn the principles of leadership, how to give a talk in sacrament meetings, how to share the gospel with others, and how to plan and participate in service activities. If you have been taught by two young missionaries you have seen the results of these programs.

Young men receive the priesthood when they are 12 years of age. As deacons they pass the sacrament. When they are 14 they become teachers and prepare the sacrament. At 16 they become priests, and among other responsibilities they bless the emblems of the sacrament. Each quorum has youth leaders and adult advisors who assist the bishop in administering the affairs of the priesthood quorums. Not only do they participate in Sunday meetings and mid-week activities, but there are also many other opportunities to serve. Just as an example, some years ago when I was superintendent of the Young Men's organization and advisor to the priests quorum my bishop called a young man to serve as his "first assistant." (The bishop is always the president of the priests quorum, but they call a young person to be their first assistant, making that young person a sort of de facto leader of the quorum). This young man was asked to be concerned not just for the welfare of the priests (ages 16 and 17), but also for the teachers (ages 14 and 15) and the deacons (ages 12 and 13). In addition the bishop also charged him with responsibility for the welfare of the young women in the comparable age groups, Laurels, Mia Maids and Beehives.

He took the assignment to heart. If members were absent, he called them to encourage them to attend. He tended to their needs if they were ill. If they had problems with the Word of Wisdom, or with living any of the other standards of the Church, he became their friend, encouraging them to participate in wholesome Church activities, and he coaxed them back into full activity. By lovingly caring for his assigned flock he acted more like a bishop than like a boy who was only 17 years of age.[7]

Our young people learn to serve in many ways. Just as another example, recently we had a huge rainstorm, the kind that happens only once in every hundred years. Basements throughout our neighborhood were flooded. We were trying to pump the water out of one of our basement rooms when suddenly three teenagers appeared. They, along with dozens of other neighbors, were roaming the neighborhood offering to help where needed. These young people are taught to minister to those who have special needs. Many of them volunteer their time to work in our local

---

7. The young man's name is Mitch Davis. He wrote and directed a wonderful movie entitled *The Other Side of Heaven* and is about to come out with another one that will be called *Stuck*. Google his name and the name of the movie and you will see what a great influence his immersion in the Church has been in his life. He is another role model for all of us.

Food and Care Coalition, preparing and serving meals to the homeless. They shovel snow from the walks of elderly neighbors. Serving others becomes a lifelong habit and blesses their lives as well as the lives of those whom they serve.

The Missionary Program

When young men reach the age of 18 and young women the age of 19, they are not required, but they are encouraged, to go on a mission. Many do, and they are great examples of how immersion in Primary and the Young Men and Young Women's programs builds character. It is more than likely that, if you are a new member, you have been taught by young men or women who have made the voluntary choice to give one and a half to two precious years of their lives to serving a mission. In many cases they have delayed the completion of their education by taking time out to serve. I admire them greatly. When the Savior was asked, "Which is the great commandment in the law?" he responded: "Thou shalt love the Lord thy God with all thy heart and with all thy soul, and with all thy mind. This is the first and great commandment. And the second is like unto it, Thou shalt love thy neighbor as thyself. On these two commandments hang all the law and the prophets" (Matthew 22:36–40). As I write these words I have four grandchildren serving on missions. During the time they will serve as missionaries they will have consecrated their lives to loving the Lord and loving their neighbor. They are typical examples of Latter-day Saint children who have been immersed in the gospel from the time of their infancy. We should strive to be like them.

Other Callings

As you know, the pattern of learning and service continues throughout our lives. As adults we attend weekly classes where we learn gospel principles and how to become Christ-like. We share our testimonies, we speak and we teach. We "home teach" and "visit teach" each other. We accept callings to serve and, in so doing, we take care of each other. And we develop close friendships with people who have similar values and goals. Attending a ward or branch is like living in a small town. Just for example, our family has moved a number of times, sometimes to different neighborhoods and sometimes to different cities or even to different states. One thing we have loved so much is that when you move to a new area and begin attending church you very quickly develop a lot of very close friends. You very quickly bond with your ward or branch members by attending church with them, by participating in activities with them, and by serving them as they serve you. Most important, your children will be likely to gain new friends and become involved in wholesome activities with new companions who have similar values.

In addition to the programs and callings I have mentioned, you have no doubt noticed that there are many others. There are ward clerks who account for the tithes and offerings and who keep the membership records up to date. There is an executive secretary who assists the bishop with paperwork and his appointments. There are Cub Scout and Boy Scout leaders, family history specialists who work with members to teach them how to do genealogy research, and the list goes on and on.

There are also callings outside the ward. There is a stake president who is like the bishop of a diocese. He is assisted by two counselors and twelve members of what is called the "high council." The high council is kind of like a board of directors. There are also stake Sunday School leaders, a stake Relief Society presidency, stake Primary presidency, stake Young Men and Young Women leaders, and stake leaders of all of the other Church organizations. Their assignment is to coordinate the activities of the ward and branch organizations and to provide instruction on a stake-wide basis.

Does all of this sound like a lot of hard work? It would be, if you had to do it all. But, remember, a typical ward is staffed by many members, male and female, young and old. And yes, it takes some effort. But it is always voluntary and never a burden. It is also a lot of fun. After all, you are doing these things in company with your closest friends. The blessings that come to us by being an active part of a ward and stake family more than compensate for any effort required or anything you may give up. Let me give you some examples.

Recently I happened to sit next to a woman at a gathering in our home following the blessing of twin babies. She was the grandmother. Her name is Joan Atkinson. She told me she had been serving as the Relief Society president in her ward for the last five years but had not always been active in the Church. Then she related the most amazing story about herself. It turns out that her story was published in the Church magazine, the *Ensign*, in 1988. With her permission I repeat it here:

"Not Me—I Smoke and Drink"

BY JOAN ATKINSON

One day about twenty-five years ago I was busy ironing and baby-sitting several children in my home. I was also enjoying a good soap opera and a cigarette.

The doorbell rang. Two men wearing business suits and warm smiles stood at the door. One of them introduced himself as the bishop of the ward. I invited them in and very quickly explained that I had been baptized into the Church when I was ten, but that I had never been very active and knew nothing about the gospel. A few months earlier I had attended a Church meeting and had put my name and address on the roll sheet, but no one had spoken to me.

The bishop smiled, looked me in the eye, and said, "I have been praying for an MIA teacher,[8] and the Lord directed me here." I told him he was out of his mind. He continued to smile, opened the lesson book he'd brought with him, and started to explain about teaching the class.

"I don't know what you're talking about," I said. "I smoke and drink. I can't teach sixteen-year-old girls."

He then explained that I was to start teaching next Wednesday at the skating rink where they

8. MIA stands for "Mutual Improvement Association" and is the former name for the Young Men's and Young Women's programs.

met for church. I kept saying, "no," and he kept right on smiling. I told him I was inactive.

He said, "Not anymore."

I said, "I smoke."

He replied, "You have until next Wednesday. God loves you. You can do it." He smiled, left the lesson book, and walked out the door. I was stunned. Then I got mad and yelled at the air, "You'd better find someone else, because I'm not going to do it!"

I tried to ignore the book, but my curiosity got the better of me. I read it from cover to cover, all twelve lessons. Wednesday drew nearer. I knew the lesson word for word. All day Wednesday I said I was not going, but at the appointed hour I pulled into the parking lot, so scared I was trembling. I had grown up in the slums, lived through gang wars, fought for food, bailed my dad out of the drunk tank, and done a stint in juvenile hall. I could fight my way out of anything, yet here I was, letting that bishop get me into a mess like this. Well, I'd show him! By this time I was sitting in the makeshift chapel and they were introducing me as a new Laurel teacher.

In the classroom, facing two angelic girls, I sat down and gave them the lesson word for word, even the parts that said "Ask the class." After the class I left quickly and went home and cried. A few days later the doorbell rang and I thought, "Oh, good, it's that smiling bishop coming after his book." But no, it was those two Laurel girls. One brought cookies, and one had flowers. They came in and taught me—about the people in the ward, about MIA, and about the class. There were sixteen girls in the class, and they hadn't had a teacher for months. Lila and Lois were the only active ones.

I liked those girls, and I agreed to go to Sunday School with them the next Sunday. They came home with me for dinner, and then we went back to sacrament meeting. We had a break between the two meetings back then.

With their help, I started teaching the other girls. If the girls wouldn't come to church, we went wherever they were. We had lessons in bowling alleys, cars, and bedrooms, and on porches. I was determined that if I needed to go to class, those girls did too. One day we were giving the lesson to a girl who was hiding in a closet, and she came out and asked, "What about my free agency?" I told her I had never heard of that lesson and that she could come and teach us the next Wednesday.

Lila and Lois became like daughters to me. They taught me to sew, to look up scriptures, and most of all, to smile.

Six months later, fourteen of the girls were coming to class, and all were active within a year. Together we learned to pray, to study the gospel, and to help others. We made many visits to the children's hospital. We laughed together

> and cried together in a bond of love. Fifteen months later, I was president of the MIA.
>
> I made a decision during that year of teaching that I would never say "no" to the bishop, and I never have. Two sixteen-year-old girls taught me that. I later learned that my smiling bishop was just as terrified of me as I was of him when he first came to my home, and he was sure I wouldn't show up to teach the class. I sure showed him—and I'm grateful!

Sister Atkinson told me how thankful she was for the bishop who followed the promptings of the Spirit by calling her to teach that class. She was especially grateful for those two young women who brought her flowers and who lovingly helped her back into activity. It moved her from what might have been a life of misery to one where she was blessed with happiness. She gained a ward family. She received instruction and guidance in how to live a happy and productive life by attending Sacrament, Sunday School, and Relief Society meetings. She met a wonderful young man and they were married in the temple for time and all eternity. With the help of her ward family she raised children who adopted her newfound values. Most important, she knows that she and her family now have the opportunity to be with each other forever. My wife and I have been similarly blessed through our membership and activity in the Church.

CHAPTER THREE

GET EVERYTHING YOU WANT

What Do We Want?

I have a hunch that most of us want to wind up with about the same things. This could include at least the following:

1. A happy marriage.
2. Obedient children with high moral standards.
3. A close social relationship with good friends who add enjoyment to our lives.
4. The opportunity to serve others and to be served in time of need.
5. A good job.
6. Good health and a long life.

7. The ability to cope with life's challenges.
8. Fun with no regrets.
9. Eternal life.

How Can We Get What We Want?

Number 1: A Happy Marriage

"Where did we come from?" "Why are we here?" "Where are we going?" These are questions we all ask. The restored gospel of Jesus Christ answers these questions with clarity. It's all about relationships—our relationships with God, with our spouse, with our children, with our ancestors, and with the entire human family.

Where did we come from? There was a great war in Heaven. It is referred to in Revelation 12:7–17. However, until I joined The Church of Jesus Christ of Latter-day Saints I never heard anything about it over a pulpit. Through the restoration we now know that we came from a preexistent state and, because we didn't rebel against our Father's plan, we have been given life with bodies and the opportunity to overcome hardships and temptations and make choices that will help us to become better people.

Why are we here? There are three degrees of heaven. They are mentioned in 1 Corinthians 12:2, where Paul speaks of a man "who was caught up to the third heaven." In the Church we refer to that third heaven as the Celestial Kingdom, the highest degree of glory. It is our goal to get there, but obviously this cannot be the result of random assignment. If it was, then those who were arbitrarily left out would have the right to complain. We believe that we are saved by grace but only "after all we can do," and that is why we are here—to seek to do our best to strive for perfection so that we might qualify for exaltation in the celestial kingdom.

Where are we going and who will we be with when we get there? The relationship between my wife and I, and our Father in Heaven and His son, Jesus Christ, is clarified through revealed scripture. In the temple we make covenants solidifying those binding relationships. As a lawyer I understand about covenants—which we lawyers refer to as "contracts." In the law we usually speak of two kinds of contracts, unilateral and bilateral. A unilateral contract is one where only one of the parties makes a binding promise. For example, I say to you, "If you mow my lawn I promise to pay you $25." You don't promise to mow it, but if you do then I am contractually bound to pay you. A bilateral contract is one where I promise to let you mow my lawn and pay you for it and you promise to mow it. We are both contractually bound.

A temple marriage is something even more. It is a "trilateral contract" where there are three parties. The couple being married makes promises to each other, and then they make promises to the third party, God, and in return God makes promises to them. I love the idea of having my Heavenly Father be a party to my marriage covenants. And I especially love the idea that if I am faithful to those covenants and other covenants we have made through priesthood and temple ordinances then He has agreed to reward us with eternal life.

The eternal nature of our marriage and the opportunity to be with each other and our family forever is a constant reminder that we must try our best to meet the other's needs. It takes the words, "until death do you part," out of the relationship. The eternal nature of our marriage motivates us to work harder to please each other. Do we ever become contentious? Of course. Over a period of more than 50 years we have found some things to disagree about and at times we have been disagreeable. But we love each other and we know that we are in it for the long run. So we "kiss and make up" and then life is good again.

Gordon B. Hinckley, who was President of the Church from 1995 through 2008, reminded us that "Marriage requires a high degree of tolerance, and some of us need to cultivate that attribute." He then quoted from a newspaper article he had clipped out and saved:

> There seems to be a superstition among many thousands of our young men and women who hold hands and smooch in the drive-ins that marriage is a cottage surrounded by perpetual hollyhocks to which a perpetually young and handsome husband comes home to a perpetually young and beautiful wife. When the hollyhocks wither and boredom and bills appear the divorce courts are jammed.
>
> Anyone who imagines that bliss in marriage is normal is going to waste a lot of time running around shouting that he has been robbed.
>
> The fact is, most putts don't drop. Most beef is tough. Most children grow up to be just people. Most successful marriages require a high degree of mutual toleration. Most jobs are more often dull than otherwise. . . .
>
> Life is like an old-time rail journey—delays, sidetracks, smoke, dust, cinders and jolts, interspersed only occasionally by beautiful vistas and thrilling bursts of speed.
>
> The trick is to thank the Lord for letting you have the ride.

On April 8, 2000, the *Los Angeles Times* reported that the divorce rate for those they described as "born-again Christians" was 27 %, that it was 24 % for non-Christians, and that Mormons who were not married in the temple and therefore presumed to be less active, had a 30 % divorce rate. They went on to say that the more active Mormons, those who were married in a temple, had a divorce rate of only 6 %.

The raw data is reported in a book entitled *Religion, Mental Health, and the Latter-day Saints*, published by the Religious Studies Center at Brigham Young University. The study analyzed the marital status of 4,858 people. It showed that 2,553 of them were married in the temple and, of those, only152 (6 %) of them were divorced. Out of the remaining 2,305 people who were not married in the temple, 705 (30 %) of them were divorced.

This study has drawn a lot of criticism, especially from those who feel threatened by our success. The critics point to the fact that 15 % of the 4858 people (which is 729 of them) were not contacted directly but instead the only data relating to them was obtained from their bishops. If a bishop didn't know about the status of a marriage he would have to get the information from Church records. But, with respect to temple marriages, these records can distort the numbers. Temple marriages are recorded in the records, but divorces do not appear in the records unless the parties seek a cancellation of the temple sealing. Sometimes people do not. To the extent that they don't, this would skew the results and lead to what appears to be a lower divorce rate among members of the Church married in the temple.

However, that is only part of the story. I have served as a counselor to two bishops and also as a bishop and a branch president. I can verify that in 90 % of the cases a bishop will know about the marital status of his ward members. If that is true, then the data for only 10 % of the 729 people would have come from church records. But, just to be more than generous to the critics, let us assume, for purposes of argument, that on average the bishops knew nothing about the marital status of any of the 729 people. So, let's do the math: Remember, 53 % of the people studied were married in the temple and 47 % were not. That means that about 53 % of the 729 names (which is 386 of them) have records that are in question.

Let us give the critics another assumption in their favor. We'll assume that 30 % of the temple-married members were divorced just like the rest of the people included in the study. 30 %

of 386 is 116. Add 116 to the 152 divorces already included in the study and you get 268 as the total of temple marriages winding up in divorce. 268 out of 2,553 means that only 10.4% of the 2,553 temple marriages studied ended in divorce. That is still only about a third as high as the divorce rate of others, which ranged from 24% to 30%.

While the divorce rate among all groups has undoubtedly risen since this study, it stands to reason that the rate of divorce among those married in the temple and who remain active in the Church is still far less than the divorce rate of others. The *Los Angeles Times* article reported on the apparent reasons why temple marriages are far less likely to wind up in divorce. They included such things as: entering into marriage with the goal that it be an eternal bond; going to the temple regularly; adhering to Church standards; avoidance of drugs, alcohol and tobacco; regular attendance at church; daily family prayer; the availability of a bishop for counseling; and regular family home evenings. I would summarize all of that with one word, "Immersion."

Number 2: Obedient Children with High Moral Standards

We learn that when we refer to God as our "Father in Heaven." The word "Father" is not just a figurative label, but that He is literally our "Father." Not only that, but He loves us dearly just as we love our own children. The predominant view of many Christian churches is the belief in a God who lacks "body, parts and passions" and is therefore viewed more as an "enforcer" than as a loving parent who weeps not just because of our sins, but also because of our sorrows.[9]

Our church does not have a monopoly when it comes to good people. There are good people of all faiths, but I know of no other organization, whether a church or otherwise, that puts as much time, effort and emphasis into building family relationships and values. We spend three hours every Sunday attending a Sacrament Meeting, a Sunday School class, and Priesthood or Relief Society sessions. In each of those meetings we learn about what kind of people we should be and we share our testimonies. We are encouraged to have daily prayer, to study the scriptures, and to have a family home evening each week. But more than that, we may participate not just as students but also sometimes as teachers. Quite honestly, sometimes a meeting may be boring, but just be patient. Soon something will be said

---

9. See Terryl and Fiona Givens' book, *The God Who Weeps*, available at Deseret Book stores. This is a book that should be in everyone's library.

in one or more of those meetings that cuts right to the heart—something that you or your spouse or one of your children needs to hear. In my case I know that sometimes I need to hear it more than once, but eventually I may get the point and become better.

Despite all of the help we receive from these church programs it is of course true that there are no guarantees that our children will all turn out to be just as we want them to be. And even though we might not want to tell our children this, there is no guarantee that we will turn out to be perfect either (although they probably know that already). We all have our free agency and we all make mistakes. Satan is very clever. He has a way of making bad things look good. Often he does that by making immediate pleasure seem more important than long-term joy and happiness. Sometimes I have thought that if we could just lock our children in the house and not send them outside, ever, we could mold them into little clones of us and then they'd be exactly what we wanted them to be without any outside influences. However, on reflection I have realized that this wouldn't work either, because we aren't perfect and we'd really like them to be better than us.

Our oldest daughter struggled with her testimony for a time and we didn't always approve of her choice of friends. But thanks to the fact that in her formative years a good foundation in the gospel had been established, and with the help of some loving ward members and a good bishop, she turned it around. At the time of her untimely death at the age of 20 due to complications of a familial disease, hereditary hemorrhagic telangiectasia (HHT), she was a devoted teacher in Primary with a strong testimony.

Our children and grandchildren are influenced by many outside forces, some good and some bad. That is exactly why we should strive to increase the impact of the good ones with the hope they may overpower the bad ones. While there are no guarantees, I am convinced that immersion in these inspired Church programs will greatly improve the odds of making them (and us) turn out better. It really helps to renew our baptismal covenants each week by taking the sacrament. It really helps to attend our Sunday meetings regularly where, no matter what our age or gender, we are taught and reminded of the values we should adopt in our lives. And it really helps us to raise our children to become Christ-like if we put them in weekly classes and activities that teach them good Christian values. It also helps us raise these children if they develop friendships with other young people who are also being immersed in those same classes and programs.

In addition, our children have benefited from Church programs that have helped us, as parents, understand our responsibilities. We were taught and encouraged to have daily prayer and weekly family home evenings with our children as they were growing up, and we attended church as a family. We have also been taught to lead by example. My wife and I do not drink alcoholic beverages. Rather than trying to teach our children "how to use alcohol responsibly," like many try to do, we teach them, by example, not to use it at all. St Francis of Assisi said "Preach always. If necessary, use words." He was right. A good example is worth a thousand words.

Our children have brought us great joy. They are typical examples of the gospel in action. They are an absolute delight, strong and faithful in the Church and hard workers. As teenagers they were our best friends and they remain so to this day. They have also given us twenty grandchildren, sixteen of them still living, and they are all good kids. Of the nine oldest grandchildren, seven of them (two girls and five boys) have served, or are serving, missions. The other two were planning on missions but they fell in love with nice young men and were married in the temple. The remaining seven grandchildren are all looking forward to going on missions. There is a lot of bad stuff out there and because of the Internet some of it even invades the privacy of our homes, computers and cell phones. We keep our fingers crossed that the grandchildren will continue to withstand the influence of Satan and remain steadfast in the faith. In the meantime, we and their parents can do nothing more than to try our best.

Number 3: A Close Social Relationship with Good Friends Who Add Enjoyment And Fun to Our Lives

It is, of course, true that immersion involves much more than just participation in worship services. As I write these words I can speak only in a whisper. I ruined my voice last night being the master of ceremonies at a ward karaoke party. We heard some very good singers, and also some very bad ones (myself included). But it was so much fun to hear the best efforts of our close friends in a setting we had not experienced before. And once the spirit of the event caught on there was a long line of cute children from ages six on up eagerly awaiting their turn to sing with visibly proud parents and grandparents looking on. Typically wards and branches will organize enjoyable activities in the middle of the week, especially for the young people so that they will develop close bonds in a fun environment.

We had another great ward outing recently—our annual salmon barbecue in a nearby park. There was something for everyone. The older people sat around and visited while the youngsters propelled themselves down a blowup slide. The highlight of it for me was when, surrounded by wide-eyed little children, I hypnotized a live Dungeness crab by rubbing its tummy and then, when it was in a comatose state, put it on my bald head until it started to wake up. For some reason those little kids want me to do that every year.

But the fun goes on even when there is no party. The Relief Society sisters love getting together each week; in fact, it takes them about a half hour just to say goodbye to each other. The teenagers meet on Sundays for their lessons and those who are called to teach do their best to make them enjoyable. Then in the middle of the week they will have a youth activity that might range from sports events, to swim parties, to weight lifting, to fishing, or to whatever their minds and the minds of their leaders can dream up.

We also seem to have a good time without drinking. A few years ago Oranee and I were asked to come up with a game to play at a gathering of lawyers and their spouses in our home town which was then Escondido, California. We were the only Mormons in attendance. After the "happy hour" where my wife and I had soft drinks and the others drank something harder, it was time for our game. We had brought two pairs of baggy long underwear and about a hundred blown up balloons. After choosing two contestants, we had them put on the long underwear over their clothing and then, over a period of three minutes, they competed to see which of them could stuff the most balloons into their underwear. We wound up with two very large and lumpy contestants, with one of them being the winner of the grand prize, a bag of candy. Afterwards one of the lawyers in attendance came up to me and said, "I didn't know this about you Mormons, but you really know how to have fun—and you do it without alcohol!"

Number 4: The Opportunity to Serve Others and to Be Served in Time of Need

Through our activity in the Church we become very close friends with fellow members of our ward or branch. Whether we are teachers or students, or serving or being served, it is enjoyable and not only brings happiness to us but to others we have grown to care about. Remember the story of Joan Atkinson. Just imagine the pleasure it brought those young girls who changed a life, and just imagine the joy and happiness it has brought to Sister Atkinson. And to go one step further, just imagine the satisfaction they felt to have influenced the lives of those Sunday School class members they were able to find and reactivate. There are times in our lives when we need help, or perhaps just to know that someone cares. In the Church we call each other "Brother" and "Sister." The fact is, because we are all children of our Heavenly Father we are indeed brothers and sisters, and because of our close association in a common cause we come to feel it even more deeply.

Number 5: A Good Job

You might be wondering how your activity in the Church can lead to a better job or financial success. I have owned a number of businesses. Let me tell you what I, and I believe every other employer, looks for in an employee: We want a hard worker, one who is honest, one who treats our customers well, one who will do a little more than is required, and one who has made or who will make, whatever sacrifices are needed to get the education or the training to do the job. I have never required that an employee be a member of my church, because there are many people who are not members of our faith who have all those good qualities. They picked them up from their parents or their friends or from their church. But I want to say it again: I know of no other organization on the face of the earth which has such a comprehensive and dedicated program for teaching those principles than The Church of Jesus Christ of Latter-day Saints.

There are people who hesitate to join the Church or who become inactive because they will need to give up some things or change their way of life. May I simply say, whatever it is you are encouraged to do, it's worth it! Just ask Joan Atkinson, the lady who resisted activity in the Church because she smoked and drank. And just think about the long-run benefits to your children and grandchildren as you lead the way, and not just with words but also by your example.

When I was about six years of age my mother was making cookies and I wanted one. She said, "No, not until after dinner." I made a very wise decision as a six-year-old. I asked, "Well then, would you put them on a high shelf where I can't reach them?" I was a smart kid. I knew my weakness for cookies and I wanted to be a good boy, so I had her put them out of reach. I not only received all the benefits that flowed from obeying my mother, but I also practiced the principle of self-discipline—something that would serve me well in later life.

When I was only twelve years of age I made another smart choice. In the church to which I and my family belonged there was no prohibition regarding the use of alcohol, but I had noticed people who staggered out of the taverns, and some of my friends told me about how their parents drank too much and sometimes even ruined family events. Therefore, I decided, at the age of twelve, to never taste alcoholic beverages. I said to myself, "Most people who begin using alcohol don't think it will become a problem, but with some people it does—and it might become a problem for me. So, if I never try it I'll never know if I like it, and if I never know if I like it I'll never want it, and if I never want it then it will never become a problem." I gave up something now for something better later on.

There are other things we give up as members of The Church of Jesus Christ of Latter-day Saints: They include pornography, premarital or extramarital intimate relationships, playing golf on Sundays, tea, coffee, alcoholic beverages, and the list goes on and on. But none of those things are that important when you compare them to the long-term blessings that follow from exercising self-discipline. I have never considered that not drinking, not smoking, not accessing pornography, abstention from sexual relationships outside of marriage, or not playing golf on Sundays was a sacrifice of anything important when compared to the blessings that flow from avoiding these things. The self-discipline our children have learned by living in accordance with the Word of Wisdom, by attending church regularly, by serving others, by living the law of chastity, and by avoiding certain kinds of movies and Internet content, spills over into other very important aspects of their lives. They are more likely to do their homework and they are more likely to save money for their education or to fulfill other long-term goals rather than spending it to meet their desire for immediate pleasure. Also, as you have seen, they even go on missions, and for two years they drag themselves out of bed each morning at 6:30 A.M. to study the scriptures, and they pound the pavement and knock on doors to find people to teach. They prepare talks for Sacrament meetings and lessons for investigators, they participate in community service projects, they give up dating for two years, and they delay pursuing their education while they serve the Lord. In the process their testimonies deepen and they learn to love and serve others.

The self-discipline they develop while serving on a mission is an asset when they return and during the remainder of their lives as they pursue educational goals and as they become employed in the business community. Self-discipline is the key to success. Winston Churchill, as a schoolboy, was one of the worst students in his class. He spoke with a stutter. Yet he went on to win the Nobel Prize for literature and became one of the greatest speakers of all time. How was he able to overcome his disabilities and handicaps to accomplish these things? Perhaps a clue to his personality is found in his words to his English countrymen when it appeared that all of Europe might fall to the advancing German troops: "We shall not flag or fail. We shall fight on the beaches, we shall fight on the landing-grounds, we shall fight in the fields and streets, we shall fight in the hills, we shall never surrender." These immortal words not only expressed a political policy, but more than that, they also are representative of Winston Churchill's bulldog determination to accomplish his goals even in the face of seemingly insurmountable odds.

The poet William Ernest Henley wrote, "I am the master of my fate, I am the captain of my soul." The sacrifice of immediate pleasure for long-term rewards is often the key to success.

A few weeks ago, in our sacrament meeting, a fourteen-year-old boy played the piano. He was incredible. I have never heard anything like it, even from a professional. He was the nephew of one our ward members and after the meeting she told us that he had given concerts in many different areas and that he practiced four hours every day.

He reminded me of the great decathlon champion, Bob Richards. When Richards was a boy he wanted to become the greatest pole vaulter in the world. He had no special aptitude for pole vaulting, or any other sport for that matter, but he had an obsession to reach his goal. As a youngster he obtained a picture of the world's greatest pole vaulter and taped it onto the ceiling over his bed. Every night he went to sleep looking at this picture and it was the first thing he saw every morning when he awoke. Later, after he had achieved his dream, he said that you can achieve anything you want if you want it badly enough—and practice 10,000 hours.

I should add that adherence to religious values also played a big part in Bob Richards' success. After a difficult adolescence and the breakup of his home by divorce, when he was 15 years of age he was taken in by a minister of a Christian church. Such a home was, obviously, immersed in the religious values of their church. In such a home he turned his life around. He attributed much of his success to "the psychological influence God exerts over those who can search their souls and find strength to perform wonderful things." Undoubtedly it was of great benefit that Richards lived in this home with an ordained minister as its head. With an ordained minister in charge, Christian values were certainly a central part of the daily lives of members of that family. And so it will be when you become immersed in the programs of the LDS Church. Whether you are a man or a woman, you are like an ordained minister in that you are asked to accept assignments to minister to members of your ward or stake, and most especially to your family. It has often been said that joining The Church of Jesus Christ of Latter-day Saints is more than just joining a church—it is a way of life. As we accept ecclesiastical responsibilities and "minister" to others, it changes our life. Like this good minister who raised Bob Richards, through activity in the Church you will develop a Christ-centered home that will bring you and your family great joy and happiness.

What was it that made this young pianist and Bob Richards successful? It was self-discipline. They had long-term goals, so while their friends were outside playing they focused on what was important to them, and they worked hard at it.

Think about it. Isn't self-discipline what distinguishes great men from the rest? Isn't that what made a Thomas Edison or a Henry Ford? Thomas Edison spent two years and tried over 6,000 fibers before achieving success with the light bulb. Henry Ford decided he wanted to develop a V-8 engine block which could be cast from one piece. His engineers said it was impossible. Ford replied, "Produce it anyway." They went to work. After a year of fruitless effort they returned to Ford and told him again that the job was "impossible." Ford's reaction was the same as before. "Go ahead," he said, "I want it, and I'll have it." They returned to their task and eventually achieved the breakthrough which led to the first practical V-8 engine.

The story of the Polaroid Land Camera is almost the same. E. H. Land, the head of the company, was told by his engineers that such a camera was impossible. So Land replied, "then I'll do it myself"—and then he did!

Members of the LDS Church generally have a reputation as ambitious, reliable, hard workers. When I got out of law school at the University of Washington I applied for a highly sought-after job as a law clerk in the Ninth Circuit Court of Appeals. There were only nine judges and therefore only nine such positions available in the eight western states that comprised the Ninth Circuit. The judge I wanted to work for and who interviewed me was an Episcopalian from Idaho. There are a lot of Mormons in Idaho and I worried that, because he hadn't joined us, he might not like us. I was near the top of my class, but not the valedictorian. My chief competitor for the job was the valedictorian of the Stanford Law School, one of the top schools in the nation. The first thing the judge said to me during my interview for the job was, "I see you are a Mormon!" I thought, "Oh no, now I'm doomed." I replied, "Yes, I am." He said, "Good, that means you are a hard worker!" I got the job.

But the benefits of self-discipline go even further. It is all about gaining the respect of others. I learned an important lesson when I was a newly baptized member of the Church. I was attending the University of Washington. I rented a room in a boarding house that went out of business. I managed to team up with five other students who were also cast out, and we found a house we could rent and share for very little money. One of them, who we barely knew before we wound up together, turned out to be just a bit unhinged. He hung a loaded shotgun on a string from the living room ceiling with the barrel pointed down so that, as air currents caused it to spin, it would randomly point at people sitting in the room. He was a good artist but drew charcoal paintings of people in various stages of death, such as by hanging or with gunshot wounds and lots of blood. You could spot one of his works of art by the fact that the dying people always had ooze dripping from their armpits. We all feared he might go berserk one night and kill us in our sleep. Anyway, he and all of my other roommates tried to get me to drink with them. They teased and ridiculed me, but I didn't give in.

At the end of the semester, when we were moving out, a most amazing thing happened. The roommate I have just described came up to me as I was leaving and said, "I just want to tell you something. I have never met anyone I respected more." Surprised to hear that from him, of all people, I asked, "why?" He replied, "Because despite all the pressure we were giving you about drinking, you never gave in—you stuck to your beliefs." He said, "I think those Mormon Church rules are stupid, but I admire you for being true to your faith."

I had a similar experience a few years later while I was in law school. I was a member of the editorial board of the *Washington Law Review and*

State Bar Association Journal, which is a scholarly treatise published by the top students of the law school. Each year there was a *Law Review* banquet. It was attended by present and former *Law Review* members as well as our law professors and the Justices of the Washington State Supreme Court. During my senior year of school I was asked to find a speaker for the banquet. I decided to try to get Jake Ehrlich, a San Francisco lawyer who was one of the greatest trial lawyers of all time. Much to my surprise he agreed.

I went to meet him at the airport with a good friend, Fred, who was another *Law Review* member but not a member of our church. We took Ehrlich to his hotel and he invited us up to his room to visit. We were, or course, thrilled with the invitation. We got to the room and Ehrlich said, "I'm going to order a Black & White scotch to drink. What would you boys like?" Fred said, "I'll have the same," and then all eyes were on me—especially Fred's. Fred knew how much I wanted to impress Jake Ehrlich. I had told him that I'd love it if I could work for Ehrlich after we graduated and learn the trade at the master's feet. I responded, "I'll just have a 7-Up." Drinks were ordered and Ehrlich told us war stories for the next two hours. It was great fun.

The next night we attended the banquet. Ehrlich told about a California Criminal Justice Commission he had helped to form and how it had proved to be of great benefit. When the dinner was over the Supreme Court Justices and some of our law professors asked if they could meet with him in the hotel bar-lounge so they could get more information about it. They thought that such a Commission might be a good thing for the State of Washington. They all headed for the door and were about to leave for the lounge when Ehrlich turned around and said, "Where's Charlie? We can't leave without him." He didn't ask for Fred. I went with them to the lounge and drinks were ordered. When they got to me I ordered my usual, 7-Up.

Ehrlich asked me to pick him up at the hotel the next morning, have breakfast with him, and take him to the airport for his plane. It was Sunday. I met him and we sat down for breakfast. He ordered a cup of coffee and I ordered a glass of orange juice. As we were eating he asked me a question: "Do you usually go to church on Sunday?" I said "Yes." He asked, "What church do you attend?" I said, "I go to the Mormon Church." He exclaimed, "I thought so!" And then he asked the BIG question: "I notice you are drinking orange juice and I am drinking coffee. Do you think less of me because

I am drinking coffee?" That was an easy one to answer. I said, "Of course not. You don't believe as I do. But if you believed as I do, then I might think less of you if you ordered coffee—because if you cannot trust yourself, how can I trust you?" He almost came out of his seat, and exclaimed, "That's what I believe!"

Before he left he asked me to look him up if I came to San Francisco and needed a job. We did move to San Francisco while I worked for a year as a law clerk, but we didn't want to live there permanently so I didn't seek a job with Ehrlich. Nevertheless, I made contact with him and became his friend. Once again, as a relatively new member of the Church I learned that people of different faiths will admire you for your steadfastness to what you believe just as we admire others who follow the tenets of their faith even though their beliefs are different than ours.

My mother and father never joined the Church, but they came to admire it. When we had our first child my mother came to Seattle to stay with us for a week so she could help us with the baby. We lived in a ward composed of married university couples. During that week many of them came to see the new baby. At the end of the week my mother said, "Your father and I have not seen such nice young people since we graduated from college many years ago. And then she emphatically continued, "No one will ever be allowed to say anything unkind about your church in my presence!" She saw, in our friends, how the Church had influenced their lives. If you are a recent convert and have family members who have questioned your decision, just be patient. There is a good chance they will change their minds when they see the good that will come of it.

Many years ago I was involved in teaching young people in priesthood and Sunday School classes. I often said to them that if I could waive a magic wand and give them a gift it would be the gift of "self-discipline." Fortunately we and our children don't need a magic wand to acquire self-discipline. We have the Church. As members we are asked to give up some things and to do some things. By doing that we acquire qualities that will help us to achieve our long-term goals.

Number 6: Good Health and a Long Life

The Word of Wisdom, as contained in the 89th section of the Doctrine & Covenants, contains a lot of good advice. But adherence to the Word of Wisdom is not easy for many new members. The use of alcoholic beverages, coffee, and tobacco can be physically addictive and it takes a lot of self-discipline to quit. I have seen that in my own family. My father smoked. At 50 years of age he finally decided to quit. It took him three tries over a period of two years before he was successful.

In addition to being physically addictive, these substances are socially and culturally addictive. Many have developed the habit of having a glass or two of wine or a cup of coffee with friends. Also, "happy hour" is common as a prelude to social gatherings. We attend them often and find that when we have our soft drinks no one is offended. In fact, I believe that, rather than being offended, and even though they might think our beliefs about that are senseless, they kind of admire us for doing what we profess to believe just as we admire and respect people of other faiths who adhere to their beliefs even though they may be different than ours. For example, I admire those of the Jewish faith, as well as the Seventh-day Adventists, who keep their Sabbath holy even though it happens to be on Saturday. I also admire those Jehovah's Witness members who faithfully come to our house every month to give me a copy of the Watchtower. They haven't been able to convert me and I haven't been able to convert them, but we always have a pleasant chat.

It is hard to put together an intelligent argument that tobacco is good for one's health. Its use is the leading cause of preventable disease and premature death in the United States. A cigarette's toxic brew of 4000 chemicals, 69 of which cause cancer, not only reaches the lungs, but also travels through the blood to tissues throughout the body, which become inflamed and damaged. Smoking causes most lung cancers and has been linked to others—from the mouth, nose and throat to a woman's cervix. It leads to plaque buildup in the arteries, which can spur heart attacks and strokes. It can make it harder for women to get pregnant and easier for anyone to develop Type 2 diabetes because the chemicals affect blood sugar.

But there are reasonable arguments that a glass or two of wine or a cup or two of coffee each day can actually be good for you. There are also reasonable arguments that they are bad for you. To me none of that matters. I have a testimony that we are led by a prophet of God. Until the prophet tells me otherwise, I won't use them. There is a lot I don't understand in this life but one thing I do understand, and that is that the Lord's prophet will not recommend any conduct that will interfere with our salvation. We can argue until we are blue in the face as to whether each and every element of the Word of Wisdom has scientific support, but one thing I know for sure: I am grateful that I and my children do not drink alcoholic beverages or smoke.

By making that decision we not only gain the benefits of full fellowship in the Church, but we avoid substances that can be harmful when used to excess or which are habit-forming. I know people who can't survive without half a dozen cups of coffee each day, and then they don't sleep well at night. I know others who can't keep the use of alcohol at a moderate level. And I am grateful that my children and grandchildren don't use it and run the risk of behaviors that sometimes seem to accompany its use.

And there is one thing I know for sure: Mormons don't have as much risk of cancer or heart disease as does the general population. Mormon men live on average seven years longer than non-Mormon men and Mormon women live on average six years longer than non-Mormon women! As far as the intellectual arguments about every element of the Word of Wisdom are concerned, those statistics are good enough for me. And while others may begin their days with a surrender to physical addictions, I like the fact that we begin our days in prayer and scripture-reading—an acknowledgment of our spiritual appetites and desires.

Number 7: The Ability to Cope with Life's Challenges

Oranee and I know something about this. Our life has not been without tragedy. I have inherited a condition known as hereditary hemorrhagic telangiectasia (HHT). It can cause nosebleeds, gastrointestinal bleeding, and life-threatening arterial venous malformations in the brain and lung. These vascular malformations, if they form in the brain, can cause strokes. If they form in the lungs they can cause oxygen deficiencies throughout the body and even brain abscesses. HHT is caused by dominant genetic abnormalities, and therefore the odds are that about 50 % of one's children will also have it.

We have had six children, two boys and four girls. Because of HHT our oldest son, Stephen, had an arterial venous malformation (AVM) in his brain which caused him to have a stroke when he was only 10 years old. It left him quite handicapped and he died 28 years later. Stephen's older sister, Patricia, developed an AVM in her lung and died at the age of 20. She was carrying a child at the time of her death, and the doctors were unable to save the child. Stephen's younger brother, Nelson, also inherited the condition. His first child died from a massive stroke only a month after she was born. They have also lost another child, but to an unrelated medical condition. Finally we lost a 13 year old grandchild who contracted meningitis, again totally unrelated to HHT. It is obvious that we have had our share, and even more than our share, of tragedies. We are often asked how we have managed to survive them all.

It was very difficult, but our testimonies of the restored gospel of Jesus Christ have helped a great deal. I will never forget the moment when it all came together for me. It was during a family gathering at the mortuary the night before the funeral for my son's month-old baby. My wife and daughters, and my son's wife, were taking turns holding the body of that little child. Our grandchildren were kind of running around and probably acting a little inappropriately, but consistent with their ages. Weary, I went to the side of the room and sat down in a chair. As I sat there taking it all in I received a witness that hardship is not only an inescapable part of life but a necessary part of life. We all face it in one way or another—and no one remains unaffected by it. Some will lose their testimonies while others will be strengthened in their faith. Elder James E. Faust of the Council of the Twelve put it this way:

> In the pain, the agony and the heroic endeavors of life, we pass through a refiner's fire. It is part of the purging toll exacted of some to become

> acquainted with God. In the agonies of life, we seem to listen better to the faint godly whisperings of the Divine Shepherd. Into every life there comes the painful, despairing days of adversity and buffeting . . . . The thorns that prick, that stick in the flesh, that hurt, often change lives that seem robbed of significance and hope. This change comes about through a refining process which often seems cruel and hard. In this way the soul can become like soft clay in the hands of the Master in building lives of faith, usefulness, beauty and strength. For some, the refiner's fire causes a loss of belief and faith in God, but those of eternal perspective understand that such refining is part of the perfection process.[10]

As I sat on the sidelines and watched my children and grandchildren I was overcome with gratitude for the blessings we had received. I was so grateful for the Plan of Salvation and the knowledge that this life is nothing more than a moment of time in eternity, and that we can all be together again if we live worthily. There is an old saying, that we should "look not at the trees, but to the forest." The trees are those difficult individual challenges we all face, whether they be financial hardships, or sickness, or accidents, or even death. The forest is the overall picture—the

10. James E. Faust, April 1979, General Conference of The Church of Jesus Christ of Latter-day Saints.

wonderful plan of salvation which gives us the opportunity, through dealing with challenges, to grow and develop so that we may merit eternal life in the Celestial Kingdom together with our loved ones.

In the preexistence a great war was fought in heaven.[11] Lucifer and a third part of the hosts of heaven rebelled against the Father's plan of salvation. They wanted salvation to come automatically to mankind without regard to the choices made during mortality.[12] Consequently, they who advocated this position were cast out of heaven, denied earthly bodies, and became the devil and his followers. I am so grateful for the increased understanding of the meaning and purpose of that great war in heaven as it has been revealed in these latter days. As I sat on the sidelines and reflected on our loss of a beloved grandchild my grief was tempered by my knowledge that the whole purpose of this life is to bring to pass our immortality and eternal life by developing Christ-like attributes. I appreciated, more fully than ever before, the fact that personal growth requires personal choice which in turn requires free agency—the power to choose. Just

11. Revelation 12:7.

12. See Isaiah 14:12-20, Luke 10:18, Revelation 12:4-13, D&C 29:36-38, Moses 4:1-4.

as we cannot develop physical muscles without lifting heavy weights, we cannot develop spiritual muscles without overcoming spiritual challenges. As Lehi said, "There must needs be opposition in all things. If not so, righteousness could not be brought to pass, neither good nor bad, neither holiness nor misery. Wherefore, all things must needs be a compound in one" (2 Nephi 2:11).

I mentioned the loss of our grandchild who died from meningitis when he was only 13 years old. He was the son of our daughter, Lisa. His name was Brady. About a year before his death I asked him what he would like to be when he grew up. His answer surprised me. I cried when he told me and I cry when I think about it. I thought he would say something like "a soccer player" or "an astronaut" or "a doctor." Instead he said, "I want to be kind. I want to be a gentle man."

Ordinarily such a response might be surprising, coming from a 13-year-old. However, when he became ill we learned that these same good qualities were not uncommon among his young LDS friends. The hospital maintained a website where our family could post daily news of his progress and where his friends could express their thoughts and hopes for his recovery. I quote from just a few of more than a hundred comments made by his young junior high school friends.

We live in Provo, Utah. In Provo most of the residents are members of the Church. The authors of these comments are all products of Latter-day Saint homes and immersion in these great church programs I have described. I have supplied only their initials because all of them are grown up now and it would be difficult to find them to obtain permission to use their names.

The following comments are typical examples of those that were posted:

> Dear Brady and Family: I just want you to know that everyone cares for you and is praying and fasting for you. "Pray 4 Brady" signs are hanging up everywhere at school and the student council handed out bracelets today that said "Pray For Brady" on them. Tomorrow a lot of people are going to fast for Brady, including me. I am even going to do it for a whole 24 hours! Our thoughts and prayers are with you! We love you! (JJ)

> Brady and Family: The countless prayers that have been said with Brady in mind have not gone unheard by our Heavenly Father. You know better than anyone what a great kid he is. Keep us updated and Brady, hang in there. My thoughts now so often turn to the good deeds he did, and all of the laughter so characteristic of Brady that could make anybody's day. Tomorrow bracelets reading "Pray for Brady" will be worn proudly by many kids. But more important, we really are praying for Brady, and we love him and all

of you, as does our Heavenly Father. To Brady, hang in there, and to his family and friends, you are having as hard a time as anyone and are not forgotten in my prayers." (KL)

Following Brady's death there were many more:

To Brady and Family: I was heart broken when I heard of your loss. I was always thinking of him through this whole time and wearing my paper "Pray 4 Brady" wrist band. I actually wore it until it was falling off because it was so ripped, but I always had him in my prayers. I can never forget him. Brady was one of the nicest people I have ever known. I could really talk to him. He had such a nice spirit about him and I never once heard him say something negative or rude to anyone. He was such a role model for me. I will miss seeing him at school, but I know that I can see him again with our Father in Heaven. He will always be in my heart. I love you, and Brady. (MO)

We love you Jensens! Everybody I have talked to says that Brady was one of the nicest people they have ever known! Today after we left lunch—me and my friends said a prayer—right in the middle of the Timpview High School commons. Even though we probably looked weird—it was one of the coolest moments of my life. Brady was such an awesome kid—he will never be forgotten. It does always seem like the nicest ones leave first and this is true with Brady. From personal experience, I know that Heavenly Father is calling

> some of his most noble spirits back to him, there must be something going on that we don't know about. Brady is going to be part of that—and I am proud to have known such an awesome kid! Especially recently, I know somewhat of the pain you are experiencing. I LOVE all of you. Brady, I will miss you—I LOVE you! (CK)

I provide these letters not just to show what a great person Brady was, but also to showcase the qualities and testimonies of the young people who wrote them. They, like Brady, are examples of what can happen when children and their families are immersed in the programs and doctrines of the Church. As members of The Church of Jesus Christ of Latter-day Saints we approach life with an eternal perspective. We understand that the purpose of this life on earth, including the hard times that sometimes befall us, is to prepare ourselves for a heavenly existence that has been made possible by the restoration of the priesthood. That will be the subject of our next chapter.

Number 8: Fun without Regrets

When I was called to be the bishop of a BYU ward some thirty years ago I drove over to the apartments that would be in the ward. It was the end of summer and most of the students had not yet returned for the fall semester. There was a young man in a pickup truck in the parking lot. I walked over to meet him and introduced myself as his new bishop. He explained that he was not really active in the ward. As we spoke I couldn't help but notice some empty beer bottles laying in the bed of the truck. I invited him to church.

When Sunday came, he was there. After the Sacrament meeting he asked to see me. It was my first interview. I don't know who was more nervous, him or me. I had been fearful that I would not know what to say to these young people if they sought advice. He explained that he was a returned missionary, and he had a question. He told me that his girlfriend, who was of another faith, had suggested they have a more intimate relationship. He said that while he had not been active and occasionally drank, he had never done what she was suggesting. But, he wondered, why not? What would it really hurt? I knew that he understood all about temple marriage and the law of chastity and what it takes to qualify for eternal life. After all, he had been a missionary. But I received an impression that what he was really wanting to know had more to do with whether there were any immediate personal rewards that would result from obedience. I believe that people sometimes respond better to immediate rewards than to distant rewards.

I was prompted to tell him that we are created in the image of our Heavenly Father. More than that, we are his children and we have the power to become like him. We are gods in an embryonic state. Being the offspring of God, we have within us the elements of divinity. Therefore, when we do the wrong thing it is inconsistent with our divine nature. We know and feel that it is wrong. It is just like when we hear a pianist hit the wrong chord. We may know nothing about how to play the piano, but we know it is wrong. I reminded him about an event that had been in the news. A whale had swum from the ocean and had entered the Sacramento River. The press nicknamed him "Humphery the Whale." Humphery was a salt water animal, and in fresh water he was dying. To save his life they had to drag him back out into the ocean where he was in his element. And so it is with us. If we engage in activities that are not compatible with our divine nature we are like Humphery the whale. It is wrong and we know it. It is like striking the wrong chord. Because it is inconsistent with who we are, we feel guilt and discomfort. The reward for obedience is happiness. He took my counsel to heart, became active, and even stopped drinking. About a year later he was married in the temple, although to a different girl.

I had another similar experience with another student. When she moved into the ward she came to see me. She didn't want to be there in my office, but her former bishop had required it. She couldn't even look at me as she hung her head in shame and told me about her past. And she concluded by saying, "I'm just no good, and I can't change." I responded, "I'm sorry, but you are lying to me." That accusation caused her to raise her head and look at me. I went on to explain: "Not only that, but you are lying to yourself! I don't see that person you have described. I see a beautiful young lady who is a child of God and who has within her the spark of divinity. You will never convince me otherwise." I told her she was a daughter of her Heavenly Father and, regardless of what she thought about herself, she was no less than divine.

She turned her life around and, rather than hanging her head in shame, when she walked into a room she brightened it up, as if a hundred light bulbs went on all at once. She was happy and acting in a way that was consistent with who she really was. Three years after she graduated and I was released, I received a letter from her. She told me she was the Spiritual Living teacher in her ward Relief Society.

The point I want to make with my teenage brothers and sisters is that there are immediate rewards from having fun while at the same time having no regrets. When we act in a way that is consistent with our divine nature we are happier. In addition there are other benefits: You get along a lot better with your parents and you may not be grounded as often. They may even let you drive.

Number 9: Eternal Life

We also have hope that after this earth life is ended there is something more. The very word, "gospel," means "the good news." And what is the good news? The Lord has said, "For behold, this is my work and my glory—to bring to pass the immortality and eternal life of man" (Moses 1:39). That includes the opportunity to be with loved ones forever instead of just "until death do you part." Ordinances performed in the temples through the power of the restored priesthood are essential—but it requires more than that. This will be the subject of the next chapter.

CHAPTER FOUR

IMMERSION AND ETERNAL LIFE

As I write these words my heart is full. Recently my wife and I were in the temple with one of our grandchildren as she was married to a nice young man for time and all eternity. With us there was another granddaughter who had recently returned from her mission in Italy, and a grandson who had just received his endowment in the temple in preparation for embarking on his mission. I was overcome with joy and had to fight back tears of gratitude as I thought about my own marriage under similar circumstances and about the eternal blessings that can be ours as a family united in love and sealed by the power of the restored priesthood.

If there is eternal life with those who went before us, how strange it would be if we did not have our immediate families with us as well. In the book of Genesis the Lord said: "It is not good that the man should be alone; I will make him an help meet for him. Therefore shall a man leave his father and his mother, and shall cleave unto his wife, and they shall be of one flesh" (Genesis 2:18, 24). I have noticed that many people of various faiths believe they will be with their families after they die, but still the official liturgy of their churches is to marry "until death do you part." That is, in effect, a bill of divorcement given them by the minister who married them, and it runs contrary to Mark 10:7–9, wherein it states, "What therefore God hath joined together, let no man put asunder." And in 1 Corinthians 11:11 Paul taught, "Nevertheless, neither is the man without the woman, neither the woman without the man, in the Lord." Certainly, as we enter into the next realm we call death and are judged by the Lord and live in his presence the man and the woman will not be without each other in the Lord.

However, even if we receive our endowments, get married "for time and all eternity" in the temple, and do temple work for our departed ancestors, that alone is not enough to give us eternal exaltation in the Celestial Kingdom. More is required. "Not every one that saith unto me, Lord, Lord, shall enter into the kingdom of heaven; but he that doeth the will of my Father which is in heaven" (Matthew 7:21). In the Doctrine & Covenants, section 88, verse 12 it states, "For he who is not able to abide the law of a celestial kingdom cannot abide a celestial glory." And as Nephi taught, "ye must press forward with a steadfastness in Christ, having a perfect brightness of hope, and a love of God and of all men. Wherefore, if ye shall press forward, feasting upon the word of Christ, and endure to the end, behold, thus saith the Father: Ye shall have eternal life" (2 Nephi 31:19–20). The key words in that passage are "press forward." We will never in this life achieve perfection but we must always "press forward," putting forth our best effort. Eternal life, which is celestial glory or exaltation, is a conditional gift: "If you keep my commandments and endure to the end you shall have eternal life, which gift is the greatest of all the gifts of God" (D&C 14:7).

It is through the grace of Jesus Christ, made possible by his atoning sacrifice, that mankind will be raised in immortality, every person receiving his body from the grave in the condition of everlasting life. But while God's grace is what ultimately saves us, it does not do so without our doing everything we can to live God's commandments. When we are baptized and receive the gift of the Holy Ghost we enter the path that leads to eternal life. But, as Nephi emphasized,

> After ye have gotten into this strait and narrow path, I would ask if all is done? Behold, I say unto you, Nay; for ye have not come thus far save it were by the word of Christ with unshaken faith in him, relying wholly upon the merits of him who is mighty to save. Wherefore, ye must press forward with a steadfastness in Christ, having a perfect brightness of hope, and a love of God and of all men. Wherefore, if ye shall press forward, feasting upon the word of Christ, and endure to the end, behold, thus saith the Father: Ye shall have eternal life (1 Nephi 312:19–20).

We also know from the prophecy of Malachi that we have responsibilities to our dead: "Behold I will send you Elijah the prophet before the coming of the great and dreadful day of the Lord. And he shall turn the heart of the fathers to the children, and the heart of the children to their fathers, lest I come and smite the earth with a curse" (Malachi 4:5–6). As stated by Ezra Taft Benson, who was then a member of the Quorum of the Twelve Apostles, "Our members need to be taught that it is not sufficient for a husband and wife to be sealed in the temple to guarantee their exaltation—they must also be eternally linked with their progenitors and see that the work is done for those ancestors. 'They without us,' said the Apostle

Paul, 'cannot be made perfect—neither can we without our dead be made perfect' (D&C 128:15). Our members should therefore understand that they have an individual responsibility to see that they are linked to their progenitors" (Regional Representatives' Seminar, 3 April 1981, p. 2).

I have an ancestor who was a protestant minister in the late 1800s. In his will he wrote, "I look forward to the day when I might be caught up into the third heaven." It was an especially touching moment when we went to the temple on his behalf and through us he received his endowments and was sealed to his wife and his children. It was an even more touching moment for me when I was sealed to my father and my mother, neither of whom were members of our church. I cannot even begin to tell you how grateful I am that someday I can be reunited with them.

I am so grateful that, because the priesthood has been restored, it is possible for us to be with our family throughout the eternities. I love my wife, my children, and my grandchildren. I miss members of my immediate family who have passed away. It will be a wonderful reunion when we can all be together again. Immersion in the programs and doctrines of the Church will help to bring that to pass.

CHAPTER FIVE

BUILDING TESTIMONY THROUGH FOCUS

There are many who argue (1) that they have conclusive evidence that our beliefs are not true, or (2) that we have no concrete evidence that they are true. Then they present what they claim is proof that we are wrong. So, how do you handle these dissident voices? Let me tell you how I handle them. There are at least five things that we can do:

1. Examine the Evidence

There is a lot of evidence for the existence of God. I am not going to even try to cover it all because the kind of evidence that will impress you depends upon your own background and experience. For me, I put great stock in witnesses. Maybe that is because I am a lawyer and am used to relying on witnesses to determine truth. I believe that Jesus was such a good person He would not lie about His divine mission. Based on scriptural accounts I believe the apostles were also good people who would not lie. Some of them testified they saw the resurrected Christ. I believe they did.

I also believe the witnesses who saw the plates from which the Book of Mormon was translated. I believe it is especially significant that even those witnesses who left the Church after disagreements with Joseph Smith stuck by their statements about the plates even in the face of ridicule.

I also view the coming forth of the Book of Mormon as nothing less than a miracle—especially coming from the mouth of an uneducated farm boy. If you, my reader, believe otherwise I would challenge you to spend the next sixty-five days creating an historical novel 531 pages long by dictating it to a scribe without using notes. While you are at it, make sure it is internally consistent within itself while it also clarifies, without contradicting, confusing Bible verses. And just to make things more interesting, put some things in it that haven't been discovered yet but which will be common knowledge 100 years from now. Then use what you have created to start up your own religion. Just so that people will know that you didn't do it for selfish reasons, give up everything for it including your life. And when you give up your life, do it knowing your likely fate, "going like a lamb to the slaughter," but "calm as a summer's morning" and with "a conscience void of offence towards God, and towards all men," just as Joseph Smith did when he left for Carthage Jail where he was killed.

I also believe that we are created in the image of God and are his children. There is evidence for that. I don't know the details of just how our Heavenly Father did it because I also believe in evolution, but one thing that convinces me about our divine nature is that if we are solely the creatures of evolution without divine intervention we wouldn't have wound up being a thousand times smarter than every other species. There would be some other form of animal life that would have progressed to a state in between us and the lowest forms of life. Think about it. Every mammal, reptile, bird and bug falls far short of humans when it comes to intelligence. If evolution results in continual development (survival of the fittest), then some of those creatures ought to be half as smart as us. But none of them are. We stand alone. None of them can invent and build a computer, a car or a cell phone. They can't read. They can't engage in abstract thought. And they don't worry about where they came from, why they are here, or where they are going. To me, that is evidence that we are indeed special—that we are children of God created with the ability to become more like Him as we progress.

Do you agree with me that the evidence I just cited about evolution is highly persuasive? It doesn't matter whether you do or don't. Like the jurors in a case, our judgment of evidence is always tainted because of our own background and preconceptions. Therefore, what impresses me may not impress you at all, and visa versa.

2. Examine the Motives of Our Critics

When evaluating the arguments of critics we should first try to understand their motives and biases. We all filter what we hear and see through our own history of experiences, our own preconceptions, and our own set of values. When we lawyers choose jurors we try to learn about their occupations, and whether they have had prior experiences that would cause them to be biased for or against the parties. The jurors will all hear exactly the same testimony and see the same exhibits, but each one will interpret the evidence differently based on his or her own preconceptions. So, the point is this: When you hear someone criticize the Church or its teachings you should always consider the source. Was the speaker angry? Did he have a competitive motive? Did he examine the evidence objectively?

The next thing I would recommend is to make sure the critic did not begin his argument with a false premise as its foundation. Often our most vocal critics will begin by defining what they think we believe and then attack that even though what they have described is not what we believe at all. I remember participating in a public debate against a member of another faith and he, good intentioned as he may have been, kept defining our beliefs erroneously before attacking them. My debate partner finally could take it no more. He interrupted one of these false descriptions of our beliefs and exclaimed: "Look, don't you tell me what I believe and then criticize it. I'll tell you what I believe and then you can criticize that!"

Generally our most vocal critics are inactive members or past members of the Church and now they want to prove they are in the right. Some of our critics may be persons who have engaged in conduct that runs counter to the Church's teachings. In such cases the only way they can justify what they have done is to convince themselves and others that the Church is wrong. Still others of our critics could be atheists who believe none of the churches are right.

Our opinions are always colored by the sum of our past experiences and conceptions. I feel strongly about this point. Like other lawyers, I have won cases I should have lost and lost cases I should have won. The American legal system is an "adversarial" system where each side has an opportunity to present the best case they can and then let a judge or a jury decide who is right. If a case is presented to a jury of twelve people there are likely to be twelve different viewpoints of the evidence. Jurors often disagree on what they believe to be the most persuasive points made. In a civil case they may vote for a party if they are only 51 % convinced that party is right and even though they are 49 % in doubt. And a party may win if only seven of the twelve vote in their favor while the five jurors who disagree with them are 99 % convinced that they are wrong. I have seldom found a case where a good argument based upon evidence could not be made for both sides. And even if one party seems to be totally guilty, he or she might be innocent and lose because the attorney is not as competent or not as prepared as the other lawyer, or because there just isn't enough good evidence available to support the case. There are times when we have to tell our clients not to even go to court because, even though they are totally in the right, they just can't prove it to the satisfaction of a jury or a judge.

Emotions play a big part in forming our opinions and in framing our arguments. I always get very distressed when I hear a party to a divorce speaking ill of their spouse. I know, based upon my experience handling such cases, that there is always another side to the story and quite often a party to such a case may be so emotionally involved that they fail to see their own faults and therefore they pin all the blame on their spouse. Sometimes a party will believe something about their spouse that is totally untrue. That could be the result of an honest mistake, or it could be the result of being so emotionally involved that they are too willing to believe an unsubstantiated rumor about their hated spouse, or it could even be the result of a desire to do harm to them and their reputation. Sometimes I reject the statements of an angry spouse without even checking the evidence because I "know" deep in my heart that they are not true.

And so it is with the arguments of critics of the Church. I "know" deep in my heart that the Church is the restored Church of Jesus Christ of Latter-day Saints. How did I come to know that? In the beginning I started by examining the evidence. The evidence was overwhelming. I studied the Book of Mormon. The doctrines clarified therein answered all of my questions and I knew in my heart that it was true. I also knew that a young man with a fourth grade education could not have come up with a Book of Mormon without divine help. He could not have known about things that weren't discovered until after he was dead. It is clear that there was a great apostasy which resulted in the loss of priesthood authority, the loss of leadership by prophets and apostles, and the loss of temples and temple ordinances, all of which have been restored. In addition there has been a restoration of baptisms for the dead and a restoration of a clear understanding of the preexistence, the purpose of life, and of eternal life with our loved ones.

3. Focus on the Major Doctrines of the Church and the Need for a Restoration

Certainly there are some critics who are not "enemies" of the Church, but who have simply found something they cannot explain in any other way except to conclude that the Church is not true. Also, sometimes those who present arguments opposing our beliefs are simply well-intentioned members of another church who feel they must prove the LDS Church is wrong in order to continue to maintain that their church is right.

I want to be clear about one thing. While I may disagree with the arguments made by members of other churches I do not mean to say or imply that they are bad people for making them. I do not mean to impugn their character when I criticize their views about our church or its beliefs. The fact is, most Christian churches are a force for good. Through their teachings they produce great people, like Mother Teresa and Billy Graham. And our Jewish friends, although they may not worship Christ or accept the New Testament, are also good examples of how we should love God and devote our lives to serving Him. One of my granddaughters spent three months in Israel as part of her college studies and upon her return she remarked, "One thing I really admire about the Jewish people is how much they remember and follow their religious values every day." She saw the goodness of the Jewish faith and its people.

The purpose of this chapter is to discuss how we should approach an analysis of the arguments made by critics of the Church. It is my experience that most often those who question the Church or its teachings are simply asking the wrong questions. Their focus is on peripheral issues that don't matter rather than upon central doctrines of the Church. I strongly recommend a book, *The Inevitable Apostasy*, by Tad R. Callister. In it he describes in detail some of the essential doctrines and practices of the early Church that are no longer accepted and practiced. Of course, it is important to understand that sometimes changes are needed. As I have explained, times and circumstances change and that is why the Lord must continue to speak to man through His chosen servants. However, I do have a problem with change when it is the result of political compromises, intellectual debate, or the philosophies of men, and especially when it results in the loss or alteration of central doctrines of the faith as taught by the Savior and His disciples.

The need for a restoration was evident. I have already mentioned the political compromises that resulted in the Nicene and Apostles' Creeds. These scholarly compromises went on for centuries, culminating in the Westminster Confession of Faith in 1646. This reformed confession of faith is in the Calvinist theological tradition. Drafted by the 1646 Westminster Assembly largely of the Church of England, it became, and remains, the subordinate standard of doctrine in the Church of Scotland and has been influential within Presbyterian churches worldwide. With various changes it has also been adopted by some

Congregationalists and even Baptists. In 1643, the English Parliament called upon "learned, godly and judicious Divines" to meet at Westminster Abbey in order to provide advice on issues of worship, doctrine, government and discipline of the Church of England. Their meetings, over a period of five years, produced the Confession of Faith, as well as a Larger Catechism and a Shorter Catechism. For more than three centuries, various churches around the world have adopted the Westminster Confession and the associated Catechisms as their standards of doctrine, subordinate to the Bible. It is significant, however, that all of these doctrinal changes have been made by scholars and philosophers who claim that God no longer speaks to men.

Our critics seldom challenge the central and basic teachings of our church and the need for their restoration. One reason is that they can't do it effectively. Instead they quibble over side issues that don't matter. A good example of this is the controversy I have already discussed involving the divorce rate of active Mormons as compared to the divorce rates of other Mormons or the members of other churches. The whole argument was based on assumed facts that weren't true, but the fact is, even if they had been defensible it wouldn't have made any difference anyway so far as our salvation is concerned. I wouldn't have wasted a day analyzing their so-called "evidence" if I hadn't been in the midst of writing this book. I did it only because I felt it was important to show how we can waste a lot of time dealing with the arguments of critics that don't relate to the central and essential doctrines of the Church that should be the real basis for our testimonies.

Let me further illustrate my point by referring to another issue that has received a lot of attention lately. Critics argue that the migrations described in the Book of Mormon, which would be from West Asia, could not have occurred because the majority of DNA identified in native peoples most closely matches the DNA of people from East Asia. The Church has addressed that issue on the Internet at "www.lds.org/topics/book-of-mormon-and-dna-studies". As is pointed out in that Internet response, the problem with the critics' arguments is that they are based upon false assumptions. They assume, for example, that no East Asians migrated to West Asia prior to Book of Mormon times despite the fact that many scientists believe that a group of such people migrated from Northeast Asia to the Americas by way of a land bridge that connected Siberia to Alaska and that these are the primary ancestors of modern American Indians. It also assumes that the people described in the Book of Mormon were the exclusive inhabitants of the Americas and therefore it would be easy to identify near Eastern DNA among the Indians. However, the Book of Mormon does not claim that the people described therein were the exclusive, or even predominant, inhabitants of the land. In fact, cultural and demographic clues in its text indicate otherwise. Also, while most geneticists believe that Native Americans belong to sub-branches of the DNA haplogroups, which are predominantly East Asian, a 2013 study indicates that as much as one-third of Native American DNA originated in Europe or West Asia and it is difficult to determine when in time such a migration would have occurred. To make matters even more complicated, casting doubt on any conclusions based upon DNA, we have no information about the DNA of Lehi, Sariah, Ishmael and others who came to the Americas. They may have inherited a genetic profile typical of areas other than those in which they lived, simply because their ancestors migrated from somewhere else and intermarried. The argument about DNA is typical of the so-called "fact-based" arguments by our critics. Often they are based on false premises or on assumed facts that aren't proven.

Sometimes critics point out that prophets are capable of making mistakes. They ask, "How could this happen if the prophet was following instructions from the Lord?" An example of such a mistake was when Joseph Smith gave Martin Harris 116 pages of his initial translation of the first part of the Book of Mormon despite the fact that God had told him not to. The pages were lost and, as a consequence, Joseph was severely chastised by the Lord. See D&C 3:3–9, which is as follows:

> 3. Remember, remember that it is not the work of God that is frustrated, but the work of men;
>
> 4. For although a man may have many revelations, and have power to do many mighty works, yet if he boasts in his own strength, and sets at naught the counsel of God, and follows after the dictates of his own will and carnal desires, he must fall and incur the vengeance of a just God upon him.
>
> 5. Behold, you have been entrusted with these things, but how strict were your commandments; and remember also the promises which were made to you, if you did not transgress them.
>
> 6. And behold, how oft you have transgressed the commandments and the laws of God, and have gone on in the persuasions of men.
>
> 7. For, behold, you should not have feared man more than God. Although men set at naught

> the counsel of God and despise his words—and he would have been with you in every time of trouble.
>
> 8. Yet you should have been faithful; and he would have extended his arm and supported you against all the fiery darts of the adversary; and he would have been with you in every time of trouble.
>
> 9. Behold, thou art Joseph, and thou wast chosen to do the work of the Lord, but because of transgression, if thou art not aware thou wilt fall.

The fact is, it doesn't matter if a prophet made a mistake or misinterpreted a supposed prompting of the Spirit. President Dieter F. Uchtdorf, in a general conference address in October, 2013, reminded us that even prophets and apostles are not infallible:

> And to be perfectly frank, there have been times when members or leaders in the Church have simply made mistakes. There may have been things said or done that were not in harmony with our values, principles, or doctrine. I suppose the Church would be perfect only if it were run by perfect beings. God is perfect, and His doctrine is pure. But He works through us—his imperfect children—and imperfect people make mistakes.

President Gordon B. Hinckley, in a media interview, was asked, "As the world leader of the Church, how are you in touch with God?"

President Hinckley responded: "I pray. I pray to Him. Night and morning. I speak with Him. I think He hears my prayers. As He hears the prayers of others. I think He answers them." The next question was, "But more than that, because you're the leader of the Church, do you have a special connection?" His answer was: "I have a special relationship in terms of the Church as an Institution. Yes." What President Hinckley was saying is that the Lord answers the prayers of all of His children, but as President of the Church he was entitled to seek guidance for the Church as an institution while other members may only be entitled to it for guidance in those areas for which they are responsible.[13]

I have only once been in the close physical presence of a prophet when he was praying. It was during the dedication of the Mormon Battalion Center in San Diego, California. There were only about fifty of us in the room. President Harold B. Lee offered the dedicatory prayer. We all reverently bowed our heads. It was the most intimate prayer I have ever heard. It was just like a conversation between two people in the same room. It was like one man speaking to his friend, and I felt the Lord was there.

---

13. *Compass*, interview by David Ransom with President Gordon B. Hinckley, aired November 9, 1997.

I wanted to look up and see Him, but it didn't seem very reverent for me to do that, especially when the Prophet was leading us in prayer only ten feet away. I fought the impulse to look around as long as I could, and finally I could fight it no more. I opened my eyes and looked. Although I was not privileged to see the Lord, I felt he was there. From this I learned that the prophet of God knew the Lord as well as I know my best friend.

That does not mean that a prophet isn't capable of misinterpreting, or even ignoring, a prompting of the Spirit. Joseph Smith did not try to hide his imperfections. He readily admitted, "I don't want you to think I am very righteous, for I am not very righteous." And, remember, President Hinckley said, "I think He hears my prayers. As He hears the prayers of others. I think He answers them." I am sure that just like the rest of God's children, there are times when our prophets "think" their prayers are answered, and other times when they "know" they are answered. I am also sure that because of their more intimate relationship with God they "know" a lot more often than do the rest of us.

When people criticize the Church for a former practice of the Church that has been modified or abandoned they will point to the change and say it is proof that God does not lead the Prophet or the Church. If He did, He would not have had to alter something He had formerly established. However, a change means nothing of the sort. For example, the temple ceremony has had a few minor changes even in my lifetime. None of them change the central message of the instructions being given, but they help us to understand what is being taught more clearly. One of the reasons the Lord needs to speak to man on a continuing basis is that times and circumstances change. What can be highly persuasive to one generation may not resonate as clearly to a later generation. For example, the Savior spoke of the wheat and the tares to make his point to an agrarian community 2,000 years ago. If He were teaching the same lesson to us today He might use something more familiar to us, such as comparing automobiles to computers.

Some of the teachings of the ancient church essential to our salvation and to our understanding of the purposes of life, which needed to be restored in their fullness, are as follows:[14]

---

14. In this section I cite to LDS scriptures clearly explaining these doctrines, and I also cite to biblical scriptures referring to the same subjects. While the scriptures from the Bible might seem clear, especially after reading the Book of Mormon, Doctrine & Covenants, and Pearl of Great Price, these biblical scriptures, as clear as they might seem, are largely ignored or misapplied by other churches, as essential doctrines have been changed.

An Understanding of the Nature of God

Earlier in this book I explained my confusion over the doctrine of the Trinity which had been developed under the direction of the Roman emperor Constantine as a political compromise between warring factions of the church. This confusion was cleared up instantly for me when I learned about the first vision of the Prophet Joseph Smith, who saw two Personages and one of them spoke to him, saying: "This is My beloved Son. Hear Him!" (Joseph Smith—History 1:16–17). The godhead consists of three separate and distinct beings with the Father and Son having bodies of glorified flesh and bones and the Holy Ghost as a spirit personage (D&C 130:22).

The teachings of the restored church help clarify many scriptures in the Bible. (See, for example, Genesis 1:26, 32:30; Matthew 3:16–17; Luke 24:39; John 5:30; 14:28; 17:21; Acts 7:55–56; Hebrews 1:1–3.) The Prophet Joseph Smith taught that "God himself was once as we are now, and is an exalted man, and sits enthroned in yonder heavens! That is the great secret. If the veil were rent today . . . you would see him like a man in form—like yourselves in all the person, image, and very form as a man" (*Teachings of the Prophet Joseph Smith*, compiled by Joseph Fielding Smith, 1976 ed., Deseret Book Co., p. 345). As the

Prophet explained, "If men do not comprehend the character of God, they do not comprehend themselves" (*Teachings*, p. 343).

Where We Came From

I know of no other Christian church which teaches that mankind lived in a preexistent state before coming to this earth. However, to understand the nature of the preexistence is to understand our relationship to God. We lived in His presence as His spirit children (D&C 138:56, Romans 8:16). God the Father provided a plan of salvation by which we could come to earth, receive bodies, and exercise our free agency to become like Him (Abraham 3:24–27). Critics who question this doctrine have a hard time explaining Jeremiah 1:5, in which the Lord told Jeremiah, "Before I formed thee in the belly I knew thee, and before thou camest forth out of the womb I sanctified thee, and I ordained thee a prophet unto the nations." (See also Hebrews 12:9, John 17:5, Job 38:1–8, Ecclesiastes 12:7.) It must be noted that in the Dead Sea Scrolls there are frequent references to pre-earth life when we all lived as spirits with our Heavenly Father.[15]

---

15. The source for this and all other references to the contents of the Dead Sea Scrolls is a book entitled *Evidences of the True Church*, by Dennis K. Brown, chapter 3. It is important to remember that

Why We Are Here

There are differing opinions among the churches as to whether man is saved by grace or by good works, or by both. The scriptures of the restored church have clarified our understanding of what is required. We are the only church to teach that, because we are spirit children of God and therefore of his species, we have the capability to become like Him. In fact, the purpose of earth life is to begin the process of eternal progression. As stated in 2 Nephi 15:23, "it is by grace that we are saved, after all that we can do." (See also Moroni 10:21.) The many biblical scriptures relating to this fundamental doctrine are thus clarified. (See, for example: Genesis 17:1–2; Matthew 5:48, 7:21–26, 10:22, 25:31–46; John 5:29; John 10:32–34; Romans 2:6, 2:13, 8:16–17; Philippians 2:12; Titus 2:14; James 2:17,19–20; Revelation 20:13, 17:22–23; Acts 17:28, Ephesians 4:12–13; Philippians 3:14–15; 2 Timothy 2:12; 2 Peter 1:3–4; Revelation 3:21, 21:7.) The Dead Sea Scrolls state that we can all progress to eventually become as a God.

---

the Dead Sea Scrolls, created somewhere between 250 B.C. and A.D. 70 were not discovered until the mid-1900s, more than 100 years after the publication of the Book of Mormon and other inspired scripture.

Where We Are Going

In 1 Corinthians 15:40–42 it is stated:

> 40. There are also celestial bodies, and bodies terrestrial; but the glory of the celestial is one, and the glory of the terrestrial is another.
>
> 41. There is one glory of the sun, and another glory of the moon, and another glory of the stars: for one star differeth from another star in glory.
>
> 42. So also is the resurrection of the dead. It is sown in corruption; it is raised in incorruption.

And despite further mention in the scriptures of a man "caught up to the third heaven" (2 Corinthians 12:2), the LDS Church stands alone in teaching about three degrees of glory in Heaven, the highest being the Celestial Kingdom where we are in the presence of Heavenly Father and Jesus Christ. The glory we inherit will depend upon the depth of our conversion, expressed by our obedience to the commandments (D&C 76:51, 74, 79, 101; D&C 107). Baptism is essential for salvation and therefore we baptize for the dead as they did in ancient times (Zechariah 9:11; 1 Corinthians 15:29; Hebrews 11:40; 1 Peter 4:6; D&C 127:5–12, 128:1–21). All persons who did not hear the gospel during mortality will have the opportunity to learn about it in the spirit world before the day of final judgment. (See Matthew

28:19; Mark 16:16; John 3:5; Acts 2:37–38, 8:12,37–38, 10:47–48, 16:14, 18:8, 22:14–16; Galatians 3:27; Titus 3:4; 2 Nephi 9:23; 31:4–12; Isaiah 24:22, 42:7, 61:1; Matthew 12:40; Luke 16:22–31; John 5:25,28, 20:17; Ephesians 4:9; 1 Peter 3:18–20, 4:6; Alma 40:12–14; D&C 138.)

Marriage Is Eternal and We Can Be with Our Families Forever

There are some references to eternal marriage in the Bible. In 1 Peter 3:7 it speaks of husbands and wives as being "heirs together" of the grace of life. And in Isaiah 65:19–25 it is stated that the Lord's elect "are the seed of the blessed of the Lord, and their offspring with them." See also 1 Corinthians 11:11 ("Neither is the man without the woman, neither the woman without the man, in the Lord"); Matthew 19:4–6 ("What God hath joined together, let no man put asunder"). It is noteworthy that in the Dead Sea Scrolls there are references to sealings to spouses and families so that they can be together for eternity.

The Difference between Salvation and Exaltation

Everyone will be resurrected with a glorified body and saved from physical death. They may also be saved from individual spiritual death through the atonement of Jesus Christ by their faith in Him and by obedience to the laws and ordinances of the gospel. There are three degrees of glory. All will be assigned to one of them based upon works. Exaltation refers to the highest degree of happiness and glory in the Celestial Kingdom (Matthew 10:41, John 14:2, 1 Corinthians. 12:3, Revelation 20:13, D&C 76).

The Restoration of Priesthood Authority

Priesthood authority was lost due to a broken line of succession, and it was restored because the ordinances of the gospel, including the blessing of babies, baptism for the living by immersion, baptism for the dead, the sacrament, blessings to those who are sick or afflicted, and temple ordinances must be performed by one having authority (Genesis 17:6; Matthew 10:16, 18:3, 19:13–15; Moroni 8:5–20; D&C 20:70; Matthew 3:16; John 3:23; Acts 8:38; Romans 6:3–5; 3 Nephi 11:23–26; Zechariah 9:11; 1 Corinthians 15–29; Hebrews 11:40; 1 Peter 4:6; D&C 127:5–12, 128:1–21; Matthew 26:22; 1 Corinthians 11:25; 3 Nephi 18:7; D&C 27:2; Numbers 27:23; Mark 8:23, 16:18; Luke 13:13; Acts 5:12, 6:3, 6:6; 8:17, 9:17–18, 13:3, 19:6, 28:8; 1 Corinthians 4:1; D&C 132, Moses 5:58–59). The Dead Sea Scrolls refer to a greater and lesser priesthood, the lesser of them being after the "sons of Aaron." They also refer to a future prophet named "Asaph," who will restore the priesthood in the last days, and who will be killed by lawless men. "Asaph," translated into English, is "Joseph."

Temple Ordinances

Temple ordinances, culminating in marriage for time and all eternity enable us to gain eternal life, conditioned also on our faith, obedience and service. (1 Corinthians 4:1, D&C 132, Moses 5:58–59). The Dead Sea Scrolls speak of the temples as being the center of life and even mention the importance of a new name, key words, special garments and a sacred oath.

Seek the Help of the Holy Ghost

If you believe in God and in His son, Jesus Christ, then you must also believe that there are some things we "know" that go beyond what we can prove with scientific evidence. According to the scriptures we are given this extra-sensory power by God himself (Alma 5:46, Moroni 10:3–5). In Acts, chapters 3 and 4, the story is told of how Peter and John healed a man who had been lame from birth. Following this miraculous cure they found many who were willing to listen to their message about Christ and His resurrection. The

Sadducees didn't like this, and they put Peter and John in prison and then the next day took them before their rulers and high priests to explain how they were able to accomplish the healing. Peter, being "filled with the Holy Ghost," explained that it was done in the name of Jesus Christ who their accusers had crucified, and that His was the only name given among men by which men can be saved. As Peter spoke, another miracle took place. These learned men to whom he was speaking cast aside all that their intellect had told them. They "perceived that they were unlearned and ignorant men, they marveled; and they took knowledge of [Peter and John], that they had been with Jesus" (Acts 4:13).

Nevertheless, even in the wake of their conversion, the Sadducees, fearing they would lose their position of power, initially decided to continue to restrain Peter and John and to forbid them to continue preaching. However, after further consideration, they decided this would not go well with those who were impressed with the miracle of healing that had been performed. They allowed Peter and John to continue to preach, and the scriptures point out that "the place was shaken where they were assembled together" and the people to whom they spoke "were all filled with the Holy Ghost" (Acts 4:31).

This is just one example of many where the scriptures teach us that through the influence of the Holy Spirit we can come to know that which is true. (See, for example, Micah 3:8, Luke 12:12, John 14:26, Alma 30:40.) When we are confirmed as members of the Church we are given "the gift" of the Holy Ghost, often referred to in the scriptures as the "Spirit," which is the right to receive His constant companionship and direction in our lives if we live worthily. The only way we can truly know something, and know it for sure, is through the power of the Holy Ghost. Both the old and the new testaments teach us that principle. (See, for example, Exodus 31:3, 36:1; Numbers 11:25; Luke 1:67; Acts 1:8, 2:17–19, 7:55, 56.)

In addition, the Book of Mormon also teaches that principle. Prayer is what influenced Alma the Younger to change his ways. Alma was actively persecuting the Saints when he was visited by an angel of God who commanded him to cease his persecutions. But even after such a vision, he still had to commit the matter to prayer. He described the process that led to his conversion: "Do ye not suppose that I know of these things myself? Behold, I testify unto you that I do know that these things whereof I have spoken are true. And how do ye suppose that I know of their surety? Behold, I say unto you they are made known unto me by the Holy Spirit of God. Behold, I have fasted and prayed many days that I might know these things of myself. And now I do know of myself that they are true; for the Lord hath made them manifest unto me by his Holy Spirit; and this is the spirit of revelation which is in me" (Alma 5:45–46). Alma's experience brings to mind the teachings of Paul: "God hath revealed [the truth of the gospel] unto us by his Spirit: for the Spirit searcheth all things, yea, the deep things of God"; "the natural man receiveth not the things of the Spirit of God: for they are foolishness unto him: neither can he know them, because they are spiritually discerned" (1 Corinthians 2:10,14).

We must always remember that the ability to receive these promptings does not come without effort. How do we merit the companionship of the Holy Ghost? It is by immersion. If we pray, read the scriptures, attend our meetings to receive regular spiritual input, do as Christ taught by loving God and serving our fellow man, and are obedient to the laws and ordinances of the gospel, the Lord has promised to give us the continual presence of the Holy Ghost. As you become immersed in the doctrines, practices and programs of the Church this will increase your sensitivity to the promptings of the Holy Spirit.

4. Recognize the Signs

How do we come to "know" something is true? Sometimes we base our beliefs on scientific evidence, at least until it changes because of newer scientific evidence. But most of the time we govern our lives by our feelings. For example, the most important decision we will ever make is to decide who to marry. We may date people, all of whom seem to be likely candidates for marriage, but then come to know in our heart that one of them is to be our eternal partner. I should add that this doesn't mean there is a guarantee the marriage will work out, because we all have our free agency to mess it up just like everything else we do in life.

Revelation does not often come as clearly as if we were seeing it on a television screen. More often it is based on a feeling deep within our heart. I remember when our youngest daughter, Alyson, then 19 years of age, was facing brain surgery because of an AVM in her brain caused from HHT. She had no symptoms, but if it were to burst at some point in her life, causing a stroke, she could have wound up with serious disabilities or even death. There were three different ways to try to fix the problem medically. She could have had embolization, surgery, radiation or a combination of some or all of them. Each choice bore its own risks, including a substantial risk of serious disability or death. She had more than one doctor and each of them had a different idea as to how to proceed. The choice was hers. To make that choice she first looked at all of the possible outcomes and risks, as related to her by the doctors. She listened to our advice, including our suggestion that maybe she shouldn't have treatment at that time. Then she prayed about it.

We learned of her decision the following Sunday, which was fast Sunday, when she bore her testimony. She said "I have prayed about it and I have decided that if the Lord wants me to join Him in the next life I am willing to go. I trust in Him and know that no matter what the outcome may be, the Lord will bless me and I will be in His care." After hearing the promptings of the Spirit, she had embolization followed by surgery. Fortunately, it was successful.

Sometimes people fail to recognize the more subtle promptings of the Spirit. Instead they wait for a "burning in the bosom" such as is mentioned in D&C 9:7–8:

> 7. Behold, you have not understood; you have supposed that I would give it unto you, when you took no thought save it was to ask me.
>
> 8. But, behold, I say unto you, that you must

> **study it out in your mind; then you must ask me if it be right, and if it is right I will cause that your bosom shall burn within you; therefore, you shall feel that it is right.**

There are some who think they can't have a "burning in the bosom" in the absence of some sort of miraculous experience. Certainly there are times when we may be given a powerful manifestation. I had such an experience in the temple one time. I was with my family and we were doing the temple work for Brady, our grandchild who died when he was only 13. At the conclusion of the ceremonies we congregated as a family in the Celestial Room. After visiting for a short time and hugging and comforting each other, it was time to leave. Everyone passed through the door to the hallway to head down the stairs and out. I was behind the others and I went out the door, but then suddenly felt the need to return and go back into the Celestial Room. This was totally unexpected. I obeyed the impulse, and just inside the door I leaned up against the wall for a moment. Suddenly I became aware of Brady's presence.

One thing that helped to confirm the reality of this experience was that it was so unexpected. I wasn't thinking about it or looking for it. But he took me by the hand and then he led me out the door, through the hall and to the top of the stairs. We went down the stairs to the first landing. I thought he would leave me, but he did not. We went down another flight to the main floor, and then much to my surprise he was gone. I am not a visionary person, and I have never had such an experience before. While I felt no flesh of a hand, I actually was compelled to hold my hand as if in a grasp. I don't know why I was privileged to feel this so strongly.

I may not have convinced you that it happened, but that is because you weren't there, and it wasn't your grandson, and only I would be privileged to know what was happening. Somehow I think the Lord, or Brady, or both of them, knew I needed the experience, and to this day I don't fully understand it. This was a sign just for me—and it was such a spiritual and personal experience that I could not speak of it for more than a month, even to my wife.

When my son was called to serve a mission he came to me and said, "Dad, I don't know what I should do. They have asked me to speak in church and I know the congregation will expect me to bear my testimony. I'm not sure I have one and I don't want to lie. What should I do?" We had a little talk and, upon further reflection, he learned that he did indeed have a testimony of some things even though he may have had unanswered questions about other things. He bore his testimony about those things he felt he "knew" in his heart were true. I must add that, after serving an honorable mission and being "immersed" in the gospel of Jesus Christ for two years, he came home with a strong testimony. He has since served as the bishop of his ward.

So, my advice to you is this: Be patient, be immersed in Church activity, and allow your testimony to grow. Douglas L. Callister, of the Seventy, in a Conference address in October, 2007, related the following story:

> When the 23-year-old Heber J. Grant was installed as president of the Tooele Stake, he told the Saints he believed the gospel was true. President Joseph F. Smith, a counselor in the First Presidency, inquired, "Heber, you said you believe the gospel with all your heart, . . . but you did not bear your testimony that you know it is true. Don't you know absolutely that this gospel is true?"
>
> Heber answered, "I do not." Joseph F. Smith then turned to John Taylor, the President of the Church, and said, "I am in favor of undoing this afternoon what we did this morning. I do not think any man should preside over a stake who has not a perfect and abiding knowledge of the divinity of this work."

> **President Taylor replied, "Joseph, Joseph, Joseph, [Heber] knows it just as well as you do. The only thing that he does not know is that he does know it."**

Of course, as you know, Heber J. Grant later was ordained a prophet.[16] This story brings to mind one from my own experience. Years ago, when our stake was being reorganized, a general authority came to Escondido, California, from Salt Lake City to make the calls. He made inquiries not only about those who were recommended, but also about others. His attention became fixed on a man who was inactive. After committing the matter to prayer he was prompted to call him to be a member of our new stake presidency. He visited the man and asked him to serve. The response was that he wasn't active and he admitted to a problem with the Word of Wisdom. The general authority asked, "Is there any reason you can't change?" He thought a minute and said, "I guess I could." The call was made and he served faithfully for many years until he became disabled from Lou Gehrig's Disease. He was one of the most spiritual men I have ever been privileged to know; the product of

16. Callister pointed out that President Grant did come to "know" the gospel was true after only a few weeks of serving in his new calling. This story came to my attention in a book by John Bytheway entitled *How Do I know If I Know?* It is a testimony-building book for the entire family.

his own immersion in the gospel. One morning, as he lay ill in his bed, he was offered a bowl of cereal and he turned it down, saying, "I will wait for the nourishment the Lord has for me." Those were among his last words. He died later that day.

5. Ignore the Critics

That's what I do most of the time, and for a number of reasons. First, when it comes to our central beliefs, which are those things that deal with our eternal destiny, I haven't found any arguments of critics that convince me. Second, when it comes to the other stuff, it is just that—"stuff" that makes no difference. If someone argues that God could not have told the pioneers to spend the equivalent of fifty million dollars in today's money to build a temple in Nauvoo, only to lose it just a few months later, I simply say to myself, "So what?" I'm not going to waste my time second-guessing what may have motivated the Lord or His prophet to do what he did. The prophet either made a mistake, or the Lord wanted to strengthen the faith of the Saints before they made their long and arduous trip west across the plains. Either way it doesn't matter. Those who question such decisions are asking the wrong questions. Instead of being occupied with side issues they ought to be examining the central doctrines of the Church and then seeking to know the truth through sincere prayer.

CHAPTER SIX

COMING TO "KNOW"

Following the death of the apostles the church was like a ship without a rudder. Without continued revelation and centralized control, each local bishop was free to do what he wanted. Wil and Ariel Durant, who wrote an encyclopedic multi-volume history entitled *The Story of Civilization*, said this: "Aside from these basic tenets, the followers of Christ, in the first three centuries, divided into a hundred creeds."[17]

The Old Testament teaches us that there was continuous revelation between God and man for 4000 years. However, it is the belief of all of the Christian churches, except for The Church of Jesus Christ of Latter-day Saints, that revelation ceased with the death of the Apostles. Apparently it is their position that all of the revelation necessary

17. Durant and Durant, *Caesar and Christ*, p. 604.

has already been given and so there is no need for modern or future prophecy. This position flies in the face of reason. There have been many changes in the world in the last 2000 years and these give us new and different opportunities to sin, new ways to spread the Lord's word, new ways to serve people, and new ways to hurt people. Our lives are very different than they would have been 2000 years ago. Are we really to believe that a loving Father in Heaven would say that He did not need to give us further advice?

In 1955 Hugh B. Brown, who in his career had been a lawyer in Canada, addressed the students at BYU. At the time he was an Assistant to the Twelve, later to become an Apostle. He spoke of a discussion he had in 1939, just before World War II, with a prominent English gentleman, a member of the House of Commons, formerly one of the justices of the Supreme Court of England:

> He called me on the phone one day and asked if I would meet him at his office and explain some phases of the gospel. He said, "I think there is going to be a war. If there is, you will have to return to America and we may not meet again." His statement regarding the imminence of war and the possibility that we would not meet again proved to be prophetic.

When I went to his office he said he was intrigued by some things I had told him. He asked me to prepare a brief on Mormonism.

I may say to you students that a brief is a statement of law and facts that lawyers like President Wilkinson prepare when they are going into court to argue a case.

He asked me to prepare a brief on Mormonism and discuss it with him as I would discuss a legal problem. He said, "You have told me that you believe that Joseph Smith was a prophet. You have said to me that you believe that God the Father and Jesus of Nazareth appeared to Joseph Smith. I cannot understand how a barrister and solicitor from Canada, a man trained in logic and evidence, could accept such absurd statements. What you tell me about Joseph Smith seems fantastic, but I think you should take three days at least to prepare a brief and permit me to examine it and question you on it."

I suggested that we proceed at once and have an examination for discovery, which is, briefly, a meeting of the opposing sides in a lawsuit where the plaintiff and defendant, with their attorneys, meet to examine each other's claims and see if they can find some area of agreement, thus saving the time of the court later on.

I said perhaps we could see whether we had some common ground from which we could discuss my "fantastic ideas." He agreed to that quite readily.

I can only give you, in the few minutes at my disposal, a condensed and abbreviated synopsis of the three hour conversation that followed. In the interest of time I shall resort to the question and answer method, rather than narration.

I began by asking, "May I proceed, sir, on the assumption that you are a Christian?"

"I am."

"I assume you believe in the Bible—the Old and New Testaments?"

"I do!"

"Do you believe in prayer?"

"I do!"

"You say that my belief that God spoke to a man in this age is fantastic and absurd?"

"To me it is."

"Do you believe that God ever did speak to anyone?"

"Certainly, all through the Bible we have evidence of that."

"Did He speak to Adam?"

"Yes."

"To Enoch, Noah, Abraham, Moses, Jacob, Joseph, and on through the prophets?"

"I believe He spoke to each of them."

"Do you believe that contact between God and man ceased when Jesus appeared on the earth?"

"No, such communication reached its climax, its apex, at that time."

"Do you believe that Jesus was the Son of God?"

"He was."

"Do you believe, sir, that after Jesus was resurrected, a certain lawyer—who was also a tent maker by the name of Saul of Tarsus—when on his way to Damascus talked with Jesus of Nazareth, who had been crucified, resurrected, and had ascended into heaven?"

"I do."

"Whose voice did Saul hear?"

"It was the voice of Jesus Christ, for He so introduced Himself."

"Then, my Lord—that is the way we address judges in the British Commonwealth—I am submitting to you in all seriousness that it was standard procedure in Bible times for God to talk to man."

"I think I will admit that, but it stopped shortly after the first century of the Christian era."

"Why do you think it stopped?"

"I can't say."

"You think that God has not spoken since then?"

"I am sure He hasn't."

"There must be a reason. Can you give me a reason?"

"I do not know."

"May I suggest some possible reasons? Perhaps God does not speak to man anymore, because He cannot. He has lost the power."

He said, "Of course that would be blasphemous."

"Well, then, if you don't accept that, perhaps He doesn't speak to men because He doesn't love us anymore and He is no longer interested in the affairs of men."

"No," he said, "God loves all men, and He is no respecter of persons."

"Well, then, if He could speak, and if He loves us, then the only other possible answer, as I see it, is that we don't need Him. We have made such rapid strides in science and we are so well educated that we don't need God anymore."

And then he said—and his voice trembled as he thought of impending war—"Mr. Brown, there never was a time in the history of the world when the voice of God was needed as it is needed now. Perhaps you can tell me why He doesn't speak."

My answer was: "He does speak, He has spoken; but men need faith to hear Him."

This was a judge speaking—a great statesman, an intelligent man. He threw out the challenge: "Do you appreciate the import of what you say?" He added, "I wish it were true. I hope it may be true. God knows it ought to be true. I would to God," he said, and he wept as he said it, "that some man could appear on earth and authoritatively say, 'Thus saith the Lord.'"

So far as I know, this English judge did not join the Church. I suspect that he may have been so highly educated that he had difficulty overcoming his preconceived ideas about religion. There are many who wonder why the Lord would choose a 14-year-old uneducated boy as the vehicle to restore His gospel. Perhaps it was because Joseph Smith was fervently seeking the truth and his mental slate was relatively clean. Also, if the Book of Mormon had come forth from some great scholar there would be many who would argue that the scholar simply wrote it. That is a hard case to make when one considers that Joseph Smith had only a 4th grade education and he dictated the Book of Mormon in only sixty-five working days without notes.

But, regardless of the evidence, the only way to "know" that the restored gospel is true is to consider the overwhelming evidence in its favor and then follow the instructions given in Moroni 10:3–4. Moroni tells us to study the Book of Mormon and then, remembering how merciful the Lord has been, ask God if these things are not true. If you do that with a sincere heart, with real intent, having faith in Christ, He will manifest the truth of it to you by the power of the Holy Ghost. For a few the answer to their prayers may come like a bolt of lightening. To most of us it is more likely to come in stages. When I first joined the Church I thought I "knew" the Church was true but now, looking back, I realize that my testimony was still in its infancy. Like the scriptures say, it has grown "line upon line and precept upon precept" as I have lived in the Church and have come to more fully appreciate the miracle of its restoration, its organization, its leadership and its doctrine. I am sure that in the few years I have remaining it will continue to grow even more. So, how do you strengthen your testimony? It is by Immersion! The more you live it the more you will love it and the more you love it the more you will feel the promptings of the Holy Ghost.

If you are a new member of the Church I strongly recommend that you do at least seven things, and do them RIGHT NOW! Doing these things will make a huge difference in your life and in the lives of your family members. And, I should add that some of the following suggestions also contain good advice (where applicable) for us long-time members and for teenagers as well.

1. Keep the Sabbath Day Holy

Attend Sacrament Meeting, Sunday School and Priesthood or Relief Society meetings every week. By doing so you will renew your baptismal covenants by partaking of the sacrament. You will receive valuable instruction to increase your knowledge of gospel principals and to help you become a better person. You will make close friends who will have similar commitments and lifestyles, and consequently they will strengthen you as you strengthen them. You will set a good example for your children, letting them know that the Church is an important part of your life.

2. Make Friends Quickly

One word of caution. Sometimes we Mormons aren't perfect. You could go to a meeting and not make new friends because our members were too bashful, or too busy, or just preoccupied. So, here is what I want you to do: You reach out to them! Extend your hand. Introduce yourself. Let them know you are new to the ward or branch, and that you are a recently baptized member. Introduce your family. In other words, make it a point to get to know people. That just might be your first (unofficial) "calling" in the new ward or branch, to teach, by example, what it means to be friendly and outgoing.

I am reminded about a story I once heard: A fellow drives his car through a small town. He sees a man sitting on his porch and so he stops and says: "I'm new to this town. How is this town? Would I like to live here?" The man responds,

"How did you like your last town?" The fellow says, "I hated it." The man on the porch says, "Well, I think you'll find this town about the same." A little while later another man drives up and stops to talk to the man on the porch. He says, "I'm thinking of moving here. Will I like this town?" The man asks, "How did you like your last town." The visitor says, "I loved it!" The man on the porch says, "Well, I think you'll find this town about the same."

So, my advice is, if you extend yourself to make friends you will find that those bashful, busy or preoccupied people will be absolutely delighted and rejoice in the fact that you are there to become immersed in their lives and the activities of the ward or branch. And if you have children, introduce them to their primary or young men's or women's leaders. Let those leaders know that you are hoping they make some close friends who will help them become comfortable in their new surroundings. If you do that, I will guarantee that these leaders will focus on your children's needs to help them become integrated into the new environment.

3. Accept a Call to Serve

There are many ways for new members to serve. You probably won't be asked to teach a Gospel

Doctrine class until you have been a member for a while, but there are many other meaningful assignments. I have served as a bishop, so as I write these words I am thinking of some typical needs that new members might be asked to fill. If you love little children, and especially if you have some of your own, there are many opportunities to serve in the Primary. We need den mothers for the Cub Scouts. We need Boy Scout leaders, basketball and volleyball coaches, home and visiting teaching supervisors, people with computer skills, ward librarians, activities leaders, sisters to help with Relief Society activities—and the list goes on an on. The beauty of it all is that quite often you will be working with experienced people who will teach you all you need to know, and you'll have fun getting to know them better.

But suppose that after a month you don't get a calling? It's real simple: Ask for one! By "asking for one" I don't mean you should seek out a specific assignment. That is for the bishop to decide after committing the matter to prayer. What I mean is, talk to a member of the bishopric. Just tell him that you have noticed how busy and active your ward members are, and you just want him to know that you would love to help out with an assignment if there is a need for it. If you need to, carry this book with you and show him the cover with the title, "Immersion," and let him know you are seeking to experience the full benefits of the Church by becoming "immersed" in the activities of the ward. Once again, even our leaders are not perfect—so make them do their jobs by putting you to work! If you approach a leader in this way they will be absolutely thrilled to learn that they have a willing and eager member who wants to serve.

4. Go to the Temple as Soon as Possible

The temple is the Lord's house, the gateway to eternal life. Within the walls of the temple you will find a peace and tranquility you will find nowhere else. In addition you will help departed ancestors begin their progression into celestial glory. While many of the temple ordinances will not be available to you until you have been a member for a year, you can begin doing baptisms for the dead right away.

As you know, you have to be worthy to enter the temple, and that is determined by the bishop after a personal interview. But this requirement is another great benefit of the temple. Because the blessings of the temples are so important, it motivates us to live our lives in such a way that we remain worthy to go there. In short, it helps to keep us on the right track.

Statistics show that new members who go to the temple soon after their baptisms are much more likely to become immersed in the programs of the Church, and to stay that way throughout their lives. I highly recommend that you speak with the bishop, tell him of your desire to do baptisms for the dead, and have an interview to receive a temple recommend. And then, go. It is very important!

5. Search Out Your Departed Ancestors by Doing Their Genealogy

The Church has the largest genealogy program in the world, and every area has specialists who are available to work with you and help you learn how to use the genealogy resources that are available. You can go to the temple without doing personal research. Names of deceased persons will be assigned to you and you can do the work for them. But it is much more meaningful for you personally if you are doing the work for a parent or grandparent or even someone further back in your family. And it is also highly interesting because you will find out things about members of your family that you didn't know.

6. Prepare for Temple Marriage

It is of utmost importance that you prepare to be married for time and all eternity in the House of the Lord. In 1897 President Lorenzo Snow said this: "When two Latter-day Saints are united together in marriage, promises are made to them concerning their offspring that reach from eternity to eternity. They are promised that they shall have the power and the right to govern and control and administer salvation and exaltation and glory to their offspring worlds without end. And what offspring they do not have here, undoubtedly there will be opportunities to have them hereafter. What else could man wish? A man and a woman in the other life, having celestial bodies, free from sickness and disease, glorified and beautified beyond description, standing in the midst of their posterity, governing and controlling them, administering life, exaltation and glory" (Lorenzo Snow, *The Deseret Weekly*, 3 April 1897, p. 481). Right away you should sit down with your bishop or branch president and have him outline what you need to do to prepare for temple marriage.

7. Find a mentor

I intended to end this section with my 6th point, above. But suddenly I felt a strong impulse to add a 7th point. Those wonderful missionaries who have taught you will be going on to fulfill their callings by teaching others. Before they do that, may I suggest that you have the missionaries introduce you to someone, perhaps a priesthood leader if you are male, or a Relief Society leader if you are female, who can help you implement the above six suggestions. Ultimately your good bishop or branch president is your mentor, but the way the Church works is that the bishop or branch president has a lot of help from other leaders in the congregation. You will not be imposing on these leaders. It's their job. For lack of a better term, let's just call the person who helps you, "your mentor." He or she, as a leader in the ward or branch will have knowledge about the resources and people who can help you become immersed in the programs I have described. For example, they can introduce you to members of the ward and stake who will assist you with your genealogy. Any calling you receive will be with the blessing of the bishop or branch president after he commits the matter to prayer, but it is always helpful for him to have the input of ward leaders such as the one who will help you to implement these ideas. They can introduce you to members of the congregation who have similar interests. They can work with youth leaders to see that your children become involved in activities of their liking and that they make friends quickly. Show the missionaries these seven steps, and have them show them to your mentor so he or she knows what you need to do and can provide encouragement and help to make it all happen.

Immersion

In The Church of Jesus Christ of Latter-day Saints we baptize by immersion. Coming forth out of the waters of baptism is symbolic of a rebirth into a new life. But in order to receive all the advantages of that new life we have to be willing to live it in accordance with the teachings of the Church. That is the central message of this book.

After your immersion into the waters of baptism, if you will then immerse yourself fully into the marvelous programs of the Church and live in accordance with its teachings, I promise you that you will be blessed beyond anything you can imagine. These days we are assaulted on every side by the enticements of the adversary. Pornography invades even our homes and computers and cell phones. Illegal drugs are readily available to those who want them. There are many movies and television shows that we are better off to avoid. While immersion in Church activities is no guarantee we will be able to withstand all those temptations,

I am very grateful that we and our children and grandchildren are immersed in programs and activities that combat these influences.

We rejoice in the opportunity to renew our baptismal covenants weekly by partaking of the sacrament. We are grateful that we can attend church once a week or more, even if it does take three hours on Sundays and even if we have to prepare a lesson or serve in some other way. Each week our brothers and sisters prepare and give lessons and talks that give us a deeper understanding of the gospel and who and what we ought to be. We appreciate the opportunity to serve others, and to be served by others in time of need. We rejoice in the fact that we have a lot of help in trying to teach our young people how to act and make good decisions that will give them happy lives.

As I complete this book it is Sunday and we just listened to general conference on television. Hearing our Church leaders speak simply reconfirmed what I already knew. We are indeed led by a Prophet who speaks for our Father in Heaven. We know that if we follow the counsel of the General Authorities we will be blessed in this life and the life to come. We are so grateful for the restoration of the priesthood and the revealed temple ordinances. We love our family and hope that we can live in such a way that we can all merit eternal life together.

In writing this book I do not want to imply in any way that being a member of The Church of Jesus Christ of Latter-day Saints is the only way to become a good person. We have many dear friends who are not members of our Church. However, as I have said, I know of no other organization, whether church or otherwise, that is so focused on helping families become better. In 1995 the First Presidency of the Church issued "The Family: A Proclamation to the World" from which I quote in part:

> In the premortal realm, spirit sons and daughters knew and worshiped God as their Eternal Father and accepted His plan by which His children could obtain a physical body and gain earthly experience to progress and ultimately realize his or her divine destiny as an heir to eternal life. The divine plan of happiness enables family relationships to be perpetuated beyond the grave. Sacred ordinances available in holy temples make it possible for individuals to return to the presence of God and for families to be united eternally. . . .
>
> Husband and wife have a solemn responsibility to love and care for each other and for their children. 'Children are an heritage of the Lord' (Psalms 127:3). Parents have a sacred responsibility to rear their children in love and

> righteousness, to provide for their physical and spiritual needs, to teach them to love and serve one another, to observe the commandments of God and to be law-abiding citizens wherever they live. Husbands and wives—mothers and fathers—will be held accountable before God for the discharge of these obligations. . . . Happiness in family life is most likely to be achieved when founded upon the teachings of the Lord Jesus Christ. Successful marriages and families are established and maintained on principles of faith, prayer, repentance, forgiveness, respect, love, compassion, work, and wholesome recreational activities.

When I received a witness that the gospel is true I felt I had to become immersed in it. I emphasize again, it is the best decision I ever made in my life, and if you do the same I promise you that it will be the best decision you will ever make in your life. It is my prayer that you will take this to heart. I ask only that, if you are inclined to do so, I would love to hear from you and have you share with me how it has all worked out for you and whether this little book has helped. My email address is charles@abbott-abbott.com. I can't promise to respond because the volume of mail may be too great—but I'll try my best. Nevertheless, I will eagerly read what you send for the simple reason that it will bring me great joy if I have helped at all.

I have a testimony that The Church of Jesus Christ of Latter-day Saints is a gift from our Heavenly Father to us in these latter days, that the restored gospel as we know it is indeed the gospel of Jesus Christ, that we are led by a Prophet of God, that the Book of Mormon, the Doctrine and Covenants, and the Pearl of Great Price are revealed scriptures, and that priesthood authority has been restored in these latter days. We are blessed to know where we came from and therefore that we are all brothers and sisters. We know why we are here and where we are going, and this tells me that it is our responsibility to join our arms together and lift each other back into the presence of our Father in Heaven.

It is my prayer that through this book I may have helped you and your loved ones, just as others have helped me and my loved ones.

One Final Thing

If you enjoyed reading this book or found it helpful, please tell others by writing a review on Amazon. The following link will take you straight to the review page:

http://www.amazon.com/review/create-review

Also, may I suggest the following books. They are an excellent source of information for new members of the Church, for people who are seeking to know more about the Church, and also for young people or less active members who are struggling with their testimony. They would make a great gift if you know someone who could benefit from them.

John Bytheway, *How Do I Know If I Know?*

Terryl and Fiona Givens, *The Crucible of Doubt*

Terryl and Fiona Givens, *The God Who Weeps*

Michael R. Ash, *Shaken Faith Syndrome*

Tad R. Callister, *The Inevitable Apostasy*

GLOSSARY OF TERMS

There are terms used in this book that are common to the Mormon culture. While they may be common words, sometimes they have meaning to us which goes beyond the usual definitions of those words as might be found in a dictionary. This glossary is added primarily for the benefit of new members of the Church so that when they hear words such as "stake house" they don't make the same mistake I made and think it refers to a "steak house." If you have a set of scriptures which we refer to as a "quadruple combination," having the Bible, the Book of Mormon, the Doctrine and Covenants, and the Pearl of Great Price, you will also find a "Topical Guide" and a "Bible Dictionary." The Topical Guide directs you to scriptures referring to certain terms and words, and the Bible Dictionary defines terms and words.

Bible: We use the King James version of the Bible, augmented by clarification from the Prophet Joseph Smith, known as the "Joseph Smith Translation."

Book of Mormon: "An account written by the hand of Mormon" and revealed to and translated by the Prophet Joseph Smith, first published in 1830.

Branch: This refers to a congregation that is not yet large enough to be a ward. It is presided over by a branch president and his counselors and is staffed by its members.

Celestial Room: The room on the other side of the veil of the temple, symbolic of the Celestial Kingdom.

Doctrine and Covenants: A book containing revelations given to the Prophet Joseph Smith and to his successors in the Presidency of the Church.

Endowment: The endowment is a temple ceremony designed to prepare participants for eternal life. It consists also of mutual covenants and promises between participants and the Lord.

Fast Sunday: The first Sunday of each month is designated as "fast Sunday" where members are asked to fast for two consecutive meals and donate what those meals would have cost for the purpose of feeding, housing, and helping to support those who are in need.

Home Teaching: Priesthood brethren are assigned one or more families to visit each month in their homes, to give them a lesson and determine whether there are any special needs that they can fill themselves, or which should be brought to the attention of the bishopric or branch presidency if even more help is requested by the family.

Pearl of Great Price: A selection of the revelations, translations, and narrations of the Prophet Joseph Smith.

Stake House / Stake Center: A stake is like a diocese. It is the organization formed to coordinate the affairs of multiple wards and branches (usually less than ten of them) within a certain geographical boundary. One of the church buildings will house the stake offices, with rooms where the stake presidency and the high council meet with each other and with members of their stake.

Testimony: A testimony is a spiritual witness given to an individual by the Holy Ghost.

Visiting Teaching: Relief Society sisters are assigned one or more sisters to visit each month in their homes, to give them a lesson and determine whether there are any special needs that they can fill themselves or which should be brought to the attention of the bishopric or branch presidency or the Relief Society president if even more help is requested by the sister.

Ward: This refers to a congregation, presided over by a bishop and his counselors and staffed by its members.

Word of Wisdom: Contained in the 89th section of the Doctrine and Covenants, this is an outline, even a commandment, regarding what we should or should not take into our bodies in order to maintain good health.